Robert Losada

RENÉ CHAR

James R. Lawler

RENÉ CHAR
The Myth and the Poem

PRINCETON UNIVERSITY PRESS

Published by Princeton University Press, Princeton, New Jersey
In the United Kingdom: Princeton University Press, Guildford, Surrey

All Rights Reserved

Library of Congress Cataloging in Publication Data will
be found on the last printed page of this book

Publication of this book has been aided by
a grant from The Andrew W. Mellon Foundation

This book has been composed in VIP Palatino

Printed in the United States of America
by Princeton University Press, Princeton, New Jersey

For Ariane and Jerome

CONTENTS

xi
Preface

1
THE MYTH

49
THE POEM

109
Bibliography

111
Index

115
List of Titles in
Princeton Essays in Literature

RENÉ CHAR

J'ai, captif, épousé le ralenti du lierre
à l'assaut de la pierre de l'éternité.

René Char

Captive, I have wedded the slow motion
of ivy to the assault of eternity's stone.

PREFACE

Over the past few years, in France and elsewhere, there has been a refound interest in Surrealism. Theses and memoirs have multiplied, specialized journals have come into existence, and for the first time some problems at the heart of the movement have been seriously broached. This is, we may be confident, only the beginning of the thorough prospection in store. Yet we may also expect critical attention to turn increasingly to the works that followed, to the reactions that Surrealism inevitably brought in its train. Subsuming the energies of the nineteen-twenties, the post-Surrealists defended themselves and established thereby diverse poetics of their own. Among such figures none appears more worthy of scrutiny than René Char, whose force of character made him come out and be separate.

This essay seeks to illustrate his evolution. In the light of his latest collection, it traces a compelling will, expressed as early as 1928, to isolate a "légende nourricière."[1] He has acknowledged the poets that became private allies in his

---

[1] "Flexibilité de l'ennui," *Les Cloches sur le cœur*, Paris, "Le Rouge et le Noir," 1928, p. 58:

La véridique histoire
De décrépitude pour régénérer
Une légende nourricière

("The authentic story / Of decrepitude in order to regenerate / A nurturing legend"). One of the most carefully elaborated poems of this first collection, "Flexibilité de l'ennur" espouses the form of Apollinaire's "Les Collines," with a parallel recourse to imagistic disorder.

quest, and one at least was clearly seminal: Arthur Rimbaud served from the start as a model of creativity, who proposed abundant lessons of style and sense in which Char discovered a source of renewal. Yet, alongside such influences, his Surrealist years were of crucial importance. Arriving in Paris from Provence at the age of twenty-two, he adhered to the movement, gave it his strong support, collaborated with Breton and Eluard on the text *Ralentir Travaux* of 1930. It was the season of a host of Surrealist activities, and Char played his part to the hilt. Enthusiastically he joined the "chercheurs d'or des rendez-vous de minuit," the "messagers délirants de la poésie frénétique,"[2] whose striving sought to unfetter language, to undim the regard of love. Surrealism's vitality seemed synonymous with his own as he published *Artine* (1930), *L'Action de la justice est éteinte* (1931), *Le Marteau sans maître* (1934) under the aegis of the Editions surréalistes. He was a precocious member of the group who devoted himself to the pursuit of the unpredictable. In 1963, thirty years after this period, he recalled his experience in grateful terms: it represented for him, as for so many of his generation, an unique perfume and image and insight—"la fleur réfractaire, la nova écumante, dont le pollen va se mêler, un pur moment, à son esprit. . . ."[3]

Nevertheless he could not but turn aside once its virtue for him was spent. If he shut no doors, a divergence took place as he gave voice to a more personal attitude to nature and art, to a refashioned poetics and thought. There were no political skirmishes with Breton, no clashes of personality; instead, he felt the parting to be a necessary progres-

---

[2] "Golden seekers of midnight encounters" ("L'Accomplissement de la poésie," *Le Marteau sans maître*, Paris, Editions surréalistes, 1934, n.p.); "delirious messengers of frenzied poetry" (*L'Action de la justice est éteinte*, Paris, Editions surréalistes, 1931, p. 27).

[3] "The refractory star, the frothing nova, whose pollen will mix, for one pure moment, with his mind" (*Recherche de la base et du sommet*, Paris, Gallimard, Collection "Poésie," 1965, p. 46).

sion. Today we realize, as we survey his writings of the middle and late thirties, that they record a dramatic struggle for supremacy within the self. Surrealist imagery recurs as a means rather than an end, for the substantial, the virile, the universal orient the poem. Char's tone is typically shrill, his confrontation vigorous. Two collections of 1938, *Dehors la nuit est gouvernée* and *Le Visage nuptial*, show the strain of an assertion that becomes at times tragic contradiction. Anxiety reigns, not from fascination with a traditional master, but with the dream language he formerly used and must now transmute. It is significant that during this struggle the *Illuminations* was seen as a privileged scripture; he would stand by the adamantine perception he held in common with Rimbaud, whom he thought ''le premier poète d'une civilisation qui n'a pas encore paru.''[4] The war years brought the inner quarrel to a climax. Poetry became a stronghold to withstand Europe's specters, which had taken on the most anguished of their shapes. Having served in the artillery in Alsace, Char returned after the defeat to his native L'Isle-sur-Sorgue; but

---

[4] ''The first poet of a civilization that has not yet appeared'' (*ibid.*, p. 130). In both *Dehors la nuit est gouvernée* and *Le Visage nuptial* Char uses a verse which does not recur in later collections; it is of a liturgical character and akin to that of Saint-John Perse in its oracular solemnity, its breadth, its drive. Thus:

> Sera-ce toujours tout bénéfice au conservateur du phare, le calendrier mis en pièces après quelque naufrage hilarant? L'homme accroupi sur ses cendres infidèles a progressé par cicatrices et monté la somme de ses pas à travers le filtre feint de son dépaysement.
>
> (Will the lighthouse keeper always draw full profit from the demolished calendar after some uproarious shipwreck? / The man crouched on his faithless ashes has advanced by scars and climbed the sum-total of his steps through the simulated filter of his disorientation).

Nevertheless Rimbaud's vision of revolution and love is written deep in these hymns. As we read in the last piece of *Dehors la nuit est gouvernée*: ''Au sein de l'arbitraire le désir débardeur de chaume rentre l'ordre de l'amour'' (''In the heart of arbitrariness desire, the discharger of thatch, gathers home the order of love'').

he was denounced to the Vichy police for alleged Communist sympathies and obliged to flee. He joined the Armée secrète, headed the Vaucluse resistance sector and, later, from 1943 to 1945, held the rank of captain—Capitaine Alexandre of the Forces Françaises Combattantes—in charge of a Parachute Reception Unit. This was a time of chaos and the absurd, and the poet's experience was one of constant vulnerability. The "hateful siege of contraries," far from being a literary stance, was lived day by day. *Feuillets d'Hypnos* (1946), his log-book of the period, articulates the values that emerged in the face of death. But the poetic harvest is seen above all in *Fureur et Mystère* (1948), wherein fierce imaginings are consigned. It is a poetry of inclemency like almost all Char has written, yet it is sustained by the moral vision of his maturity. The twin slopes of roughness and temperance are not resolved or rounded off, since each qualifies the other in a fruitful discomposure. It is understandable that Camus should have recognized in Char a brother-at-arms and that he counted *Fureur et Mystère* among the finest of modern poetry.

In 1950 *Les Matinaux* confirmed Char's mastery. Here were songs of his moments of great good fortune, "ailes de communication" between his quietude and fever.[5] Death is not forgotten, but contained in morning exultation; a scar is an integral part of the lyric. The contemporary plays *Claire* (1949) and *Le Soleil des eaux* (1951) are parallel allegories of man's contact with nature, of mortality as the needful counterpoint of life, of the enduring virtues of the heart. They find their culmination in *La Paroi et la Prairie* (1952) and *Lettera amorosa* (1953) in which sensuality combines with abstraction, reticence with passionate drive, to produce some of his most fervent writings.

The later works show growing disenchantment with the century: Char's protests are violent, his aphorisms severe. Yet his allegiance is constant to certain central images such

[5] *Les Matinaux*, Paris, Gallimard, Collection "Poésie," 1974, p. 23.

as the violence of lightning-flash, the attentiveness of the rose. He strove to resume the sense of his work by way of *Poèmes et Prose choisis*, dated 1935 to 1957, which spells out the constancy of his values. A second anthology, *Commune Présence* (1964), went still further in offering a summum of eight main clusters of poems going back beyond *Le Marteau sans maître* and forward to unpublished collections. All dates are, however, rigorously excluded, chronological order disregarded, so that the pieces figure a presence whose apparent evanescence is firm ("Cette fumée qui nous portait"). Alongside these books several shorter collections were published: *La Parole en archipel* contains poems written from 1952 to 1960; *Le Nu perdu*, 1964 to 1970; *La Nuit talismanique*, 1955 to 1958, and 1972; and *Aromates chasseurs*, 1972 to 1975. Each has its particular climate and tone, finding in the act of creation both seed and consummation. Thus the archipelago of poems is not dispersion but hidden continuum; loss becomes nakedness reclothed; the night of suffering has a magical bearing. Finally, in *Aromates chasseurs*, Char affirms his recommitment to nature, his exorcism of stagnation, the exemplary encounter of opposites in the name of Orion.

All these collections possess exceptional variety of forms; they rejuvenate language as they develop multiple avenues of expression. In this task Char has been served by intimate acquaintance with the full body of French poetry since the Middle Ages—from the liturgical to the profane, from regular verse to prose. "Heavy with a thousand years of poetry,"[6] as he once described himself, he has constituted an œuvre whose most evident trait is a stylistic discontinuity that demonstrates its properly erotic force. The poet is he who "gives joy to words,"[7] who engenders the furious movement, the prodigal instant, the

[6] *Arrière-histoire du poème pulvérisé*, Paris, Jean Hugues, 1972, p. 27.
[7] "Donner joie à des mots . . ." (*Faire du chemin avec . . .* , Avignon, Librairie "Le Parvis," 1976, n.p.).

redemptive substance. In the first part of this brief study I shall attempt to delineate the myth that has guided Char's poetry for forty years. It finds its elaboration in his latest collection, yet nowhere in sequential manner, for poetic time determines a ritual without beginning or end. The aim is to create the rhythm of ceaseless desire, the luminous image of energy wherein reside man's strength and the wellspring of his revolt. His myth is not inert but diversely potent: it is a structure in which he reads his vibrant response. From the mid 'thirties he envisages a goal that over and again he must attain. The trajectory each time needs to be discovered, and it is never final; a moment will conjoin the personal and the collective, the sudden and the durable. He has lived through hardships, known "eclipses" and "returns," but his language holds to a lasting appetence. Brevity is written into the myth, and an ineluctable transiency, because none is less naive than this man who perceives what his century has wrought. His post-Surrealist work indicates, however, at the nub of his rebeginnings, the continued fertilization of an essential scheme. Having described this pattern of the imagination, I shall consider the plaquette *La Paroi et la Prairie*, which Char wrote in his forties. The ten short pieces are typical of their author, and paradigmatic of a work that is a summit of French poetry since Apollinaire. His bestiary will, then, be examined in detail with a view to showing what I hold to be the splendor of its diction, its robust yet manifold dynamic, above all, its visionary symbolism in which wall and prairie epitomize the unresolved tension of his mature writings.

The approach can be termed oblique in the first part, direct in the second, but the principal emphasis throughout is on close reading. Although this method is not much favored by today's avant-garde, it allows us more than any other, I think, to enter the semantic thickness, to engage the quiddity of the poem. This is of course vital when we choose a work as dense as Char's. Yet there are other modes of criticism I find pertinent in discussing these texts, such as the thematic, the mythological, the moral, and they are here put to use. My attitude, however—new critical theory being so much changed—must be deemed traditional: the readings are underpinned by continuous reference to a sensibility, a reason, a will—those of the poet himself, whose myth of desire is inextricably bound to his drama of creation.

It is a pleasure to acknowledge my indebtedness to René Char for his generous welcome; to the commentators of Char, especially Georges Blin, Maurice Blanchot, Virginia A. La Charité and Mary Ann Caws, whose newly published book is a landmark; to François Chapon of the Fonds Doucet; to Albert Sonnenfeld; to Jerry Sherwood of Princeton University Press; and to Wayne State University Press, the publishers of *About French Poetry from Dada to Tel Quel: Text and Theory*, ed. Mary Ann Caws (1974), for permission to reproduce a modified version of my study "René Char's *Quatre Fascinants*." I am also happy to state my warm thanks to the John Simon Guggenheim Memorial Foundation for the fellowship that enabled me to write this essay.

By kind permission of the copyright-holders Editions Gallimard, the following texts are quoted in their entirety: "Hommage et famine," "Le Bouge de l'historien," and "J'habite une douleur" from *Fureur et Mystère*, © Gallimard, 1949; "Les poings serrés . . . ," first collected in *Placard pour un chemin des écoliers*, GLM, 1936, from *Poèmes et Prose choisis*, © Gallimard, 1957; "Débris mortels et Mozart" and "La Paroi et la Prairie," from *La Parole en archipel*, © Gallimard, 1962; "Commune Présence," first collected in *Le Marteau sans maître*, José Corti, 1934, from *Commune Présence*, © Gallimard, 1964; "Dyne," from *Le Nu perdu*, © Gallimard, 1971; and "Ebriété," from *Aromates chasseurs*, © Gallimard, 1975. The translations are my own.

Halifax, Nova Scotia   J.R.L.

The Myth

Published in 1976, *Aromates chasseurs* treats the paradox of herb and hunter, that which is sought and that which seeks, the ambrosial and the kinetic. The two dozen texts are warm with thyme and sage, yet their richness is not sufficient unto itself but the sign of a way beyond. Char indicates what he calls a third space vital for him amid ruinous assaults on being. As he has written: "J'ai cherché dans mon encre ce qui ne pouvait être quêté: la tache pure au delà de l'écriture souillée."[1]

In taking up themes that have accompanied a long career, the collection proposes Orion as the central image. Without a linear anecdote the mythical figure gives substance to disparate forms. Its sense is plurivalent, weaving a dialogue with its object of desire in a manner that recalls Rimbaud's gospel of Genius; nevertheless Char does not proclaim a demiurgic poet or any other single creator but an idea of beauty, a vision by which he can live and act— "comme une barque incontinente au-dessus des fonds cloisonnés."[2] Violence, tenderness, death and transmutation characterize the poems just as they mark the fable of

---

[1] "I looked in my ink for that which could not be sought: the pure spot on the far side of tainted writing" ("A une sérénité crispée," *Poèmes et Prose choisis*, Paris, Gallimard, 1957, p. 260). On the cyclical movement into and out of the demonic realm, see Northrop Frye: *The Secular Scripture: A Study of the Structure of Romance*, Harvard University Press, 1976. Frye calls the imagery of the hunt a theme of descent ("The consummation of the hunt is the death of the animal, which for Actæon is the turning of the pursuer into the victim"); but in Char the ascent is an integral part of the myth, the complementary pattern of an action that is never completed once and for all.

[2] "Like an incontinent boat over the partitioned depths" ("Faction du muet," *Le Nu perdu*, Paris, Gallimard, 1971, p. 28).

Orion, who suffered blindness and defeat despite his strength yet who, in death, shines with stellar splendor. The antipoles of height and depth are tokens of the dramatic tension. All of us, says Char, are in a free fall; we are in the process of being unmade as surely as we were made, as precipitately as Lucifer fell from heaven. Yet in this fall there is a point of rest, a depth that at last is reached: "Après la chute interminable, nous gisons écrasés sur le sol."[3] Now can appear—"Haute est sa nuit"—a salvational guide.[4] Orion reveals the brilliance of nature ("Il tend son arc et chaque bête brille . . . "),[5] the dowry of love (" . . . la renouée des chemins devant sa chambre nuptiale . . . "),[6] the marvelous invigoration of art like Rodin's bourgeois of Calais ("Aujourd'hui la lyre à six cordes du désespoir que ces hommes formaient, s'est mis à chanter dans le jardin empli de brouillard . . . "),[7] the bridges of thought he anxiously wishes to build for himself and his fellow men ("Il faut deux rivages à la vérité: l'un pour notre aller, l'autre pour son retour . . ."). [8] Thus may Orion be resurrected and time's tyranny overcome. The myth relates to a period that builds with steel no less than to the Golden Age, its universality as broad as the title of one of the most resonant poems of the series, "Orion iroquois"; for Char is drawn by the knowledge that in the cosmology of the Iroquois the date of the Midwinter ceremonial was set by observing the Pleiades, with which the constellation of Orion is associated. Across cultures, and across apparently hermetic

---

[3] "After the endless fall, we lie crushed on the earth" ("Lombes," *Aromates chasseurs*, Paris, Gallimard, 1975 [1976], p. 21).
[4] "Deep is his night" ("Réception d'Orion," *Aromates chasseurs*, p. 27).
[5] "He bends his bow and each beast shines" (*ibid.*).
[6] "The knotgrass of paths before her nuptial chamber" ("La Dot de Maubergeonne," *Aromates chasseurs*, p. 28).
[7] "Today despair's six-stringed lyre which was formed by these men has begun to sing in the foggy garden" ("Rodin," *Aromates chasseurs*, p. 30).
[8] "We need two shores for truth: one for our going, the other for his return" ("Pontonniers," *Aromates chasseurs*, p. 32).

eras, an encounter occurs that causes him to ask: "Devant
l'horloge abattue de nos millénaires, pourquoi serions-
nous souffrants? Une certaine superstition n'ennoblit-elle
pas?"[9]

The book of poems also contains the image of the lark
celebrating the harvest and, at the same time, the climax of
youth. Joy is at its fullest, the moment intoxicating; yet
death is at hand as autumn follows summer, as mirror and
gun make ready to kill the bird that resembles some mortal
god:

> Tandis que la moisson achevait de se graver sur le
> cuivre du soleil, une alouette chantait dans la faille du
> grand vent sa jeunesse qui allait prendre fin. L'aube
> d'automne parée de ses miroirs déchirés de coups de
> feu, dans trois mois, retentirait.[10]

Char expresses no pathos but the enactment of a drama
destined to take place and, as clearly, to begin again. We
are led to set aside the view of his work as fragmentary and
to find instead a concrete logic, a unitary imagination. Certainly a first reading of *Aromates chasseurs* would appear to
belie this: the reader is confronted with seemingly discrete
passages that elude narrative order; but we discern in
the fragments—"brefs éclairs qui ressemblent à des
orgasmes"[11]—constant tension with a code that not only

---

[9] "Before the overthrown clock of our millennia, why would we be suffering? Does not one kind of superstition dignify" ("Orion iroquois,"
Aromates chasseurs, p. 37); cf. "Comment ne pas conserver derrière son
oreille, pour assurer la continuité du muguet, le brin de thym écarlate de
la superstition" (*Arrière-histoire du poème pulvérisé*, p. 28). "How is one not
to keep behind one's ear, to ensure the continuity of the lily-of-the-valley,
superstition's twig of scarlet thyme?"

[10] "While the harvest engraved the last touches of its image on the cop-
per of the sun, a lark in the fault of the huge wind sang of its youth about
to end. In three months' time the autumnal dawn would ring out, decked
in its mirrors shattered by gunshots" ("Ebriété," *Aromates chasseurs*, p.
31).

[11] "Brief flashes that resemble orgasms" ("Arthur Rimbaud," *Recherche
de la base et du sommet*, p. 127).

interanimates this plaquette but reveals in retrospect, as I wish to show, the implicit mythopoeic convergence of the whole. I shall first examine the role of nature, which is of directly personal significance; then love; then art; and, finally, the underpinning philosophical stance instinct with tragic awareness. Surrealism served as a point of departure but his poetry finds a compelling focus of its own, an intense commitment to moral issues, a hope born of despair. He affirms the enduring sense of a viaticum, to which today he gives the name of Orion. He can follow the hunter, his fall halted, his task incomplete, as he designates again the third space of insurrectionary desire.

Aromates chasseurs speaks to us, then, with freshness. In particular, title and imagery recall the landscape of Vaucluse, where Char has spent practically all his life. One has seen the fields by his home purple with lavender; in similar fashion, Vaucluse gives his collection a summer radiance—a quality not unique to *Aromates chasseurs* but here vigorously achieved.

In reading him from his origins, we grow familiar with the "closed valley" (*vallis clausa*), a good number of whose place-names occur throughout his work. The river Sorgue, the wood of the Epte, Venasque, the Thor, Buoux, the Lubéron, the summits of Montmirail, the Ventoux: these are features of a countryside with which he has communed. He associates them first and foremost with his childhood in L'Isle-sur-Sorgue when nature was a refuge from early apprehensions: "J'avais dix ans. La Sorgue m'enchâssait. Le soleil chantait les heures sur le sage cadran des eaux."[12]

Yet it is not only field and rock he attends to, but a multifarious animal life. "Le peuple des prés m'enchante. Sa

---

[12] "I was ten. The Sorgue enshrined me. The sun sang the hours on the waters' sage dial" ("Déclarer son nom," *Commune Présence*, Paris, Gallimard, 1964, p. 3).

beauté frêle et dépourvue de venin, je ne me lasse pas de me la réciter."[13] Vaucluse is the region of lark and swift, snake and cricket, and he introduces them into his poetry. He also refers no less frequently to grass, flowers, trees, harvest. Established in his youth, a correspondence between a lively nature and the self still prevails, so that the one can seem to be the mirrored reflection of the other:

> Champs, vous vous mirez dans mes quatre moissons.
> Je tonne, vous tournez.[14]

When we look back to his beginnings as a poet, however, we see a nature of small consistence. The evocations in his first collection *Les Cloches sur le cœur* were caught in a screen of literary models, and the murmur of reality was distant. His starting-point is not the real but a heady mixture of anxiety and irony. An uninvolved moon presides; the heart is inescapably gauche; and the self seeks escape—"Clown musical"—in Laforguian masks. In the next several years allusions to nature were even less precise when he "came up" to Paris, turned to Surrealism, and gave himself to the exploration of dreams. *Le Marteau sans maître* of 1934 brings together the main compositions of this period and shows how far he had traveled along the dim byways of fantasy and pathos ("la fausse aurore dallée de fossiles célestes et de bissacs de larmes"),[15] with what ardor he had sought self-knowledge. But the years 1935 and 1936 were a watershed that removed him further and further from André Breton's position. He observed what he took to be the abortive procedures of Surrealism,

---

[13] "The people of the fields enchant me. I do not tire of reciting to myself their frail beauty devoid of venom" ("Feuillets d'Hypnos," *Poèmes et Prose choisis*, p. 55).

[14] "Fields, you are mirrored in my four seasons. / I thunder, you turn" ("Captifs," *Commune Présence*, p. 14).

[15] "The false dawn paved with celestial fossils and pouches of tears" ("Tous compagnons de lit," *Dehors la nuit est gouvernée*, Paris, G.L.M., 1949, p. 42).

gauged their debility at a time of Europe's moral collapse. And nature—an illness having forced him to return to Vaucluse—became a domain to be reconquered. The Provençal landscape, its mountains and meadows, had to be learnt afresh. A major step in this relearning is consigned in a fragment of 1936 that he chose twenty years later as the epigraph of a volume of poetry and prose:

Les poings serrés
Les dents brisées
Les larmes aux yeux
La vie
M'apostrophant me bousculant et ricanant
Moi épi avancé des moissons d'août
Je distingue dans la corolle du soleil
Une jument
Je m'abreuve de son urine[16]

That he should give such prominence to these lines emphasizes their importance: nature was no longer a thing to be discerned darkly, but now a generative force. Moreover, the words he uses implicitly echo the myth of Orion whose conception as formulated in Greek popular etymology was by way of the urine of the gods. The concreteness of the images, the combined violence and sensuality, the energetic rhythms turn Char in a different direction from that of his Surrealist years. On the one hand, he indicates the sufferings and snares of a life thirty years old; on the other, his appetency is full-blooded in a way that Surrealism did not permit. The ear of corn would yet ripen; Orion would lead the hunt.

The history of his subsequent writings can in one sense be described as his increasing awareness of nature, the

[16] "Her fists clenched / Her teeth broken / Her eyes filled with tears / Life / Reproaching me, hustling me, and sneering / —I the early ear of corn of the August harvests / —I discern in the sun's corolla / A mare / I quench my thirst in its urine" (*Poèmes et Prose choisis*, p. 9).

realization of its symbolic truths. A detail is never merely a picturesque object but is both emblem and teaching. "Ce pays," he writes, "n'est qu'un vœu de l'esprit, un contre-sépulcre";[17] again, in Parnassian style:

Et qui sait voir la terre aboutir à des fruits,
Point ne l'émeut l'échec quoiqu'il ait tout perdu.[18]

The reader is not slow to recognize the nourishing power henceforth inscribed in his work. Man, beast, plant, earth enjoy a "common presence" that allows erotic convergences: rock calls to figtree ("Figuier, pénètre-moi: / Mon apparence est un défi, ma profondeur une amitié"),[19] lizard to goldfinch ("Léger gentil roi des cieux, / Que n'as-tu ton nid dans ma pierre!").[20] There is also—no longer a poem of Vaucluse but of southern Provence, where Char stayed in 1946 with Henri Matisse—the admirable "Le Requin et la Mouette." As its first paragraph shows, it is an illuminated conceit, the nuptials of shark and gull, the discovery of a hidden music:

Je vois enfin la mer dans sa triple harmonie, la mer qui tranche de son croissant la dynastie des douleurs absurdes, la grande volière sauvage, la mer crédule comme un liseron.[21]

Out of the imagined meeting of bird and fish comes not

[17] "This countryside is but a wish of the mind, a counter-sepulcher" ("Qu'il vive!," *Commune Présence*, p. 9).

[18] "And he who can see the earth coming to fruit / Is not moved by defeat although he has lost all" ("Redonnez-leur . . . ," *Poèmes et Prose choisis*, p. 111).

[19] "Fig-tree, penetrate me: / My appearance is a challenge, my depth a friendship" ("Les Transparents," *Commune Présence*, p. 186).

[20] "Slight and courteous king of the skies, / Why don't you nest in my stone!" ("Complainte du lézard amoureux," *Poèmes et Prose choisis*, p. 124).

[21] "At last I discover the sea in its triple harmony, the sea that beheads the dynasty of absurd pains with its crescent, the great wild aviary, the sea as credulous as a bindweed" ("Le Requin et la Mouette," *Poèmes et Prose choisis*, p. 80).

one, nor two, but a magical three: the poem follows a ternary development in its paragraphing as well as in its triple naming of the elements of harmony that resemble the spectra obtained by diffraction. No attempt is made to compose a representational portrayal like that of Matisse in his series of drawings on the same theme; instead, the poet "sees" with his imagination and his lucid desire. In the first lines he postulates a junction of redemptive powers: the sea despatches darkness, imposes wildness, affirms itself as innocence, loyalty, trust; it is scimitar, bird, convolvulus; at one and the same time sovereign violence, savagery, submission. The second paragraph, however, changes this triad into a personal deliverance: *"j'ai levé la loi, j'ai franchi la morale, j'ai maillé le cœur."*[22] Corresponding to each of the initial terms, Char's words offer an abstract reading of the same images—fatal law has been rejected, inert codes transgressed, irresponsibility tamed. The poet is thereby released from his past as on the first day of creation, fortified by resources he can presently tap. Now, yet again, a triadic formula is developed: "Ainsi, il y a un jour de pur dans l'année, un jour qui creuse sa galerie merveilleuse dans l'écume de la mer, un jour qui monte aux yeux pour couronner midi".[23] Adding to the renewal previously affirmed the new images denote purity, marvel, crowning brightness, each lit with the clarity of an instant illumination. But the poem ends on quite a different note: a prayer is addressed to the vision of shark and gull in the hope that it may serve as a loadstar: "Faites que toute fin supposée soit une neuve innocence, un fiévreux en avant pour ceux qui trébuchent dans la matinale lourdeur".[24] We observe a

---

[22] "I have revoked the law, I have traversed morality, I have netted the heart" (*ibid.*).

[23] "So there is one pure day in the year, a day that drives its marvelous gallery in the sea's foam, a day that rises with our gaze to crowning noon" (*ibid.*).

[24] "Let every supposed end be a new innocence, a feverish forward-march for those who stumble in the morning sultriness" (*ibid.*).

triad complementary to those already evoked which recalls the curved sword, the simple plant, the intense myriad of birds, yet here seen less as a triumphant discovery of what has already taken place than as an accomplishment never realized once and for all. The nuptials the poet speaks of quicken his energy, his moral sense, his imagination, but under pain of death they remain of necessity ideal.

Thus, in moments of insight, Char finds nature to be an efficacious talisman. Orion cannot content himself with his prize but must advance, opening a path; so animals and prairie engage in a dance of desire—bird with bird ("oiseaux chasseurs d'autres oiseaux"),[25] flower with herb ("Un aromate de pays / Prolongeait la fleur disparue");[26] and the poet too, both hunter and prey, participates in the round. A flower can find him unguarded, its beauty suddenly redounding to his strength:

Courte parvenue,
La fleur des talus,
Le dard d'Orion
Est réapparu.[27]

It is, however, not easy to determine where love begins and nature ends. Each is bound to each, the arrow of beauty inseparable from sensuous delight.

[25] "Birds hunters of other birds" ("Les Parages d'Alsace," *Commune Présence*, p. 225).

[26] "A native aromatic / Continued the vanished flower" ("Les Trois Sœurs," *Commune Présence*, p. 57).

[27] "Swiftly come, / The flower of the slopes, / Orion's dart / Has reappeared" ("Jeu muet," *Le Nu perdu*, p. 75). "Le dard d'Orion," as the poem indicates, is the name given to a small flower of Vaucluse. It will be plain that Char can in no sense be called a bucolic poet. One of the central aspects of his crisis in the 'thirties was his struggle with the temptations of romantic solitude in the bosom of nature. As he wrote in *Dehors la nuit est gouvernée* of 1938:

Qui n'entend que son pas n'admire que sa vue
Dans l'eau morte de son ombre.   ("Remise")
(Who hears only his step, admires his view alone / In the dead water of
    his shadow.)

L'été et notre vie étions d'un seul tenant
La campagne mangeait la couleur de ta jupe odorante[28]

Love is desire as innocent as eating and breathing, the experience of intimate collusion between a couple and the elements.

C'était au début d'adorables années
La terre nous aimait un peu je me souviens[29]

In the absence of a divine being the milieu proffers its sign of election, so that to look back on such a moment when it has passed is to feel no nostalgia, but gratitude. Nevertheless, unlike nature, whose importance for Char grew dramatically after 1935, love is at the center of his Surrealist period as of the later work. In the anthology of his writings published in 1964 he included three poems from *Le Marteau sans maître* in the section "Haine du peu d'amour." The first two, "Tu ouvres les yeux . . . " and "Voici," are short hymns to sexual love ("O ma diaphane digitale!" "O caresses savantes, ô lèvres inutiles!"),[30] the third, a coolly precise epigram on the name of Sade ("Comme gel sous l'eau noire, sommeil fatal, crapaud").[31] We are sensitive to the lapidary character of these pieces which eschew the personal for the general; yet, however clear the vision, poetic power is realized at the expense of the moral distance of his maturity. A fourth text even more revealing of the early poet is "Artine."[32] The name suggests a connection between woman and art, which the dedication underlines:

[28] "Summer and our lives were of a single piece / The countryside ate the colour of your perfumed skirt" ("Evadné," *Poèmes et Prose choisis*, p. 37).
[29] "It was at the beginning of wondrous years / The earth loved us a little I remember" (*ibid*.).
[30] "Oh my transparent digitalis!"; "Oh knowing caresses, Oh useless lips" (*Commune Présence*, pp. 76, 81).
[31] "Like frost beneath black water, fatal sleep, toad" ("Sade," *Commune Présence*, p. 111).
[32] *Le Marteau sans maître*, Paris, Corti, 1953, pp. 23-25.

"Au silence de celle qui laisse rêveur."[33] Written when Char was twenty-three, it expresses in clear prose a sexual and spiritual thirst and the answer to thirst. In the eyes of the poet-rider who pursues the ideal, Artine is both "sécheresse monumentale" and "transparence absolue"—a glass of water, an inexhaustible freshness, a calm. Adopting the language of religious paradox, Char evokes flame without smoke, shadow without darkness, motion without mobility: "édredon en flammes précipité dans l'insondable gouffre de ténèbres en perpétuel mouvement" but also "sans fumée, présence en soi et immobilité vibrante."[34] At the end of the text the poet kills his model but the idea survives, since Artine is of mystical essence and sacred force, the genesis and goal of poetry.

I take "Artine" to be significant for Char's later development in that it discovers by means of an elusive love the unassailable mystery of art; it will continue to be for him throughout his long career, as he wrote to Yvonne Zervos concerning L'Action de la justice est éteinte, "ce lointain bûcher toujours renaissant" ("this far-off funeral-pyre ever rekindled")—the imperious, constantly invigorating statute of eroticism. The mode is allegorical, the language verging on disembodiment, but Char will continue to treat his theme in other forms and with greater sensuousness. He had, however, first to go to the limits of Surrealist explorations, completing an excursus that absorbed several years. When he would wish to go no further, it was the offices of love that ensured his return and brought a rejuvenated creation. Implicit in Le Marteau sans maître, the crisis attains its grand articulation in "Le Visage nuptial" of 1938.[35]

[33] "To the silence of her who leaves us in reverie."
[34] "Eiderdown of flames cast into the fathomless gulf of perpetually moving shadows"; "smokeless, self-encompassing presence and vibrant immobility."
[35] Poèmes et Prose choisis, pp. 33-36. For a detailed and incisive reading of "Le Visage nuptial," see Mary Ann Caws: The Presence of René Char, Princeton University Press, 1976, pp. 171-192.

The poem is composed of fifty-nine verses, or "versets," divided into twelve sections that Char patently elaborated with exceptional care. The first movement comprises four groups of verses, a second six, a third two, and these establish a pattern of their own (5, 6, 5, 6; 4, 7, 5, 6, 7, 4; 6, 2). A discipline is found whereby the paragraphs modify one another, control the flow of emotion, force self-awareness. The vocabulary is rich in terms taken from nature, particularly images of space ("jour," "ciel," "azur," "étoile," "espace," "horizon"), that are placed alongside a gamut of abstract words among which predominate the -ance and -ence suffixes denoting present continuity ("renaissance," "assistance," "Présence," "dissidence," "conscience," "permanence," "survivance"). So we find on the surface level of language a dual recourse to nature and abstraction which creates a verbal tension such as Char nowhere developed in his Surrealist poems. More striking still is the syntax: all is directed toward intensity by the use of the second person singular and plural, nine imperatives and half a dozen virtual imperatives, a multitude of vocatives, enumerations, parallelisms. We hear—or rather over-hear—a struggle of factions within the self, the excitement of a gradual liberation.

In the sequence of his text the poet comprehends that love works a reversal that is less a rejection of the past than its acceptance in another form. His plenitude of desire is at once founded on a tonic lucidity and the awareness of an intimate wound or ill.

> Et moi semblable à toi
> Avec la paille en fleur au bord du ciel criant ton nom,
> J'abats les vestiges,
> Atteint, sain de clarté.[36]

[36] "And, like you / With the flowering straw on the edge of the sky calling your name, / I overthrow the traces, / Wounded by light, luminously whole" (*ibid.*, p. 33).

The last line is crucial. The wound is the obverse of the "plaie de corsaire" of night which the poet's Surrealist adventure showed him (Section 6), the terrible bite of its eagle—"flux des lésions inventives," again "La pioche de l'aigle lance haut le sang évasé" (Section 5)—but also the mediating spell of the woman—"Mon souffle affleurait déjà l'amitié de ta blessure" (Section 7). He is, then, harmed but whole; more correctly no doubt, he is made whole, enriched, by the very consciousness of his harm. His former companions are left behind and he is reborn, having chosen presence against vaporousness, love's limits against limitless breadth, life against false intimations of immortality.

> Je boise l'expédient du gîte, j'entrave la primeur des
>   survies.
> Embrasé de solitude foraine,
> J'évoque la nage sur l'ombre de sa Présence.[37]

This is the space in which one can live, a sure and solid ground, an almond enfolding the future tree. Rebirth is taking place, which is of the nature of a miracle long prepared: the "charroi lugubre / De voix vitreuses, de départs lapidés," the "micas du deuil" are the heralds of a "vitre inextinguible"; "la servitude qui se dévore le dos" is answered by the woman's "royauté apparente," in the same way as the poet's wound becomes its own luminous likeness. Descending to a bottommost point like the men of *Aromates chasseurs*, the self can return: "Je touche le fond d'un retour compact."[38] But nothing is lost: the streams of shadow and death add their nourishment to the waters, past mysteries emerge into day, imagination ascends to a fertile plateau. Where before a solitary destiny was in

---

[37] "I prop the device of the shelter, I impede the first fruits of survivals. / Ablaze with itinerant solitude, / I evoke the swimming on the shadow of her Presence" (*ibid.*, p. 34).
[38] "I touch the depths of a compact return" (*ibid.*, p. 35).

jeopardy, the poet proclaims "l'intime dénouement de
l'irréparable"—a clearness that corresponds to the sky, a
permanence that partakes of silex. No longer sole individ-
uals, the lovers have become exemplary:

> Voici le sable mort, voici le corps sauvé:
> La Femme respire, l'Homme se tient debout.[39]

"Le Visage nuptial" breaks decisively, then, with Char's
previous love poems not merely by the central role given to
natural imagery, nor by its splendid sensuousness (one
cannot but recall the invocation to sex: "O voûte d'effusion
sur la couronne de son ventre, / Murmure de dot noire! / O
mouvement tari de sa diction! . . ."),[40] nor by its artistic
control, but, commanding these, by its moral seriousness.
Char expresses a turning-point in his existence that allows
him to encompass past, present and future. At the age of
thirty-one he reviews his development, opts for awareness, assumes his destiny. Love finds nature to accompany
it, but also art, which is the privileged means of making
experience universal. In "Artine," it is true, love and
poetry were already one, and this was a marvellous gift;
here likewise they are synonymous with grace, but also
endurance, perspicuity, virtue, redemption. "Orion, charpentier de l'acier?" we read in *Aromates chasseurs*, "Oui, lui
toujours; et vers nous. La masse d'aventure humaine passe
sous nos ponts géants."[41]

   Yet if "Le Visage nuptial" is one of Char's most moving
texts, *Lettera amorosa*, published in 1953, is of still greater
force and must, I think, count among the finest love poems

---

[39] "Here is the dead sand, here the body saved: / Woman breathes,
Man stands erect" (*ibid.*, p. 36).

[40] "Oh vault of effusion on the crown of her belly, / Murmur of dark
dowry! / Oh the drained movement of her diction! . . ." (*ibid.*, p. 34).

[41] "Orion, carpenter of steel? Yes, ever he; and toward us. The mass of
man's adventure passes under our giant bridges" ("Orion iroquois,"
Aromates chasseurs, p. 37).

in French.[42] Several traits echo the earlier composition, such as the imagery of the desert, the central hymn to sexual love, the alchemical dissolution of an ill. But Char's pattern is now fully orchestrated, the tone less shrill, as purification is counterpointed by the elegiac passage of time: fugitive bird will lead to harvest, fall to summer, night to dawn. Less than a change of vision, we find an artistic authority that justifies the Monteverdi title and epigraph ("Non è gia part'in voi che con forz'invincibile d'amore tutt'a se non mi tragga")[43] whereby the composition takes a rightful place in the high tradition of impassioned song.

It comprises forty-five paragraphs of poetic prose and one seven-line verse gloria. There is also a marginal summary in the fashion of medieval allegory that finds the sense of the whole, the good chance, largesse, riches revealed by deprivation, the victory wrenched from defeat: "Le cœur soudain privé, l'hôte du désert devient presque lisiblement le cœur fortuné, le cœur agrandi, le diadème."[44] At the end a second annotation of a different kind occurs under the heading "Sur le franc-bord"—the free-board being the terrain left unencumbered along the edge of a river or, as here, skirting the text. This consists of a series of definitions of the word "Iris" only slightly modified from Littré, which concludes with Char's indication: ". . . Iris plural, Iris d'Eros, Iris de *Lettera amorosa*." The page does not supply snippets of additional information like those Eliot gave with some humor for *The Waste Land*; on the contrary, Char's notes are precious in that, taking up the natural, the scientific, the mythological, the tradi-

[42] *Commune Présence*, pp. 133-144.
[43] "There is no part of you that does not draw me wholly to it with an invincible force of love."
[44] "His heart suddenly deprived, the host of the desert becomes almost readably the fortunate heart, the heart expanded, the diadem."

tionally poetic ("Nom propre de femme, dont les poètes se
servent pour désigner une femme aimée et même quelque
dame lorsqu'on veut taire le nom," Char writes, echoing
Littré),[45] he states their joint relevance to the work, re-
minding us of the intrinsic ambiguity of all poetic language; at the same time he suggests a special plurality in
this poem whose Iris—rainbow, goddess, messenger, mistress, planet, butterfly warning of death, the eye of the beloved, the small yellow flower of rivers—is as multiple as
love itself.

We realize the organic importance of "Sur le franc-
bord," as that of the single marginal annotation, the epigraph, the title pointing to a musical tradition; each performs a similar function of stylization. Moreover, this
strategy marks not only the points observed, but the structure of the entire text. Of significance in this regard are the
first three paragraphs that form the introductory movement. Printed in italics, they serve from the start to emphasize distance of time and place—although distance is
here not detachment—and they announce the resolution
that will be achieved in the body of the poem. Thus the
first paragraph affirms that suffering will bear fruit:

> Temps en sous-œuvre, années d'affliction. . . . Droit
> naturel! Ils donneront malgré eux une nouvelle fois
> l'existence à l'Ouvrage de tous les temps admiré.[46]

With abstract dynamism Char designates a tension between present and future, travail and procreation, natural
right—identified ironically with pain—and the artwork he
envisages in terms of alchemy. Already direction and goal
are confidently stamped with the seal of victory.

[45] "Woman's proper name, which poets use to designate a mistress and
even some lady whose name they wish to conceal."
[46] "Time of buttressing, years of affliction . . . Natural right! They shall
in spite of themselves again give life to the Work admired from age to
age" (ibid., p. 135).

In the second paragraph the focus changes as the language of love is introduced:

> Je te chéris. Tôt dépourvu serait l'ambitieux qui resterait incroyant en la femme, tel le frelon aux prises avec son habileté de moins en moins spacieuse. Je te chéris cependant que dérive la lourde pinasse de la mort.[47]

The plain words of commitment occur twice as the poet addresses the woman, and both times they are made more telling by an accompanying image that evokes that which would contradict love. Woman is freedom and without her man is entrapped; she is the enemy of death, although her love makes us all the more alert to death's ponderousness. The use of repetition, the metaphorical language, the exact rhythmical balance of the two halves of the second sentence, the assonance, alliteration and inversion of the third, create effects wholly different from the previous lines and produce by implication the sense of wonderment that sustains the poem.

The last lines offer yet another perspective in that they recall love and the meaning it contains as if it were long past, as if—we might conjecture—it were a planet viewed from afar.

> "Ce fut, monde béni, tel mois d'Eros altéré, qu'elle illumina le bâti de mon être, la conque de son ventre: je les mêlai à jamais. Et ce fut à telle seconde de mon appréhension qu'elle changea le sentier flou et aberrant de mon destin en un chemin de parélie pour la félicité furtive de la terre des amants."[48]

[47] "I cherish you. Soon destitute would be the ambitious man without belief in woman, like the hornet at grips with his gradually reduced skilfulness. I cherish you while the heavy pinnace of death pursues its drifting."

[48] " 'It was, blessed world, in such a month of thirsty Eros, that she lit the body of my being, the conch of her belly: I confused them thereafter.

Here, instead of a promise or a declaration, we have the confession of experience. The poet speaks of what he knows, his words a lyrical transcription of a particular event. Abstract terms do not suffice, however, nor metaphors of hornet and boat, but only the language of religious fervor in which thirst is answered by blessing, destiny by felicity; and the parallel construction of the two sentences ("ce fut . . . tel mois . . . qu'elle illumina . . . ," "Et ce fut à telle seconde . . . qu'elle changea. . . .") shows the sudden penetration of body and mind by the action of light. In similar fashion, "le sentier flou et aberrant" becomes "un chemin de parélie," the aureole of love that augurs man reborn—"déjà mi-liquide, mi-fleur"—and dawn's final radiant·resurgence.

So we have in these opening lines the sense and substance of *Lettera amorosa*. The motifs are introduced, the themes stated in the manner of a musical composition. Now all has been said, but there remains the symphonic elaboration Char executes with constantly shifting focus. At no time is the attitude allowed to solidify into the moroseness of a lover far from his mistress. The discontinuous text is not only a defense against bombast; it figures Char's conception of love that the persona of *Lettera amorosa* expresses in these terms: "Je ne puis être et ne veux vivre que dans l'espace et dans la liberté de mon amour."[49] Space and freedom: thus is defined the condition he postulates in order to counter the lovelessness that absence would impose. The sphere of love coincides with the third space of Orion, a future uncircumscribed, an expanse open to renewal. If we understand separation in these terms, we discover its magical meaning as an extraction that turns loss to gain:

And it was at such an instant of my apprehension that she changed the blurred and aberrant path of my destiny into a parhelion way for the furtive happiness of the land of lovers.' "

[49] "I can only be, and only wish to live, in the space and freedom of my love."

Et la douleur qui vient d'ailleurs
Trouve enfin sa séparation
Dans la chair de notre unité[50]

Pain is transformed into splendor; absence illuminates the undivided body of love.

Varying in tone from the casual to the elevated, *Lettera amorosa* asserts, and reasserts, the poet's fidelity to an ideal—respect for woman, imperious desire, refusal of self-pity. Like the author of "Le Visage nuptial," he accepts the wound inflicted in order that, refining it, he may be whole. There can be no question of blinding himself to pain: "Affileur de mon mal je souffre . . . ";[51] but summer will return and its triumph can be celebrated exultantly:

Amour hélant, l'Amoureuse viendra,
Gloria de l'été, ô fruits!
La flèche du soleil traversera ses lèvres,
Le trèfle nu sur sa chair bouclera,
Miniature semblable à l'iris, l'orchidée,
Cadeau le plus ancien des prairies au plaisir
Que la cascade instille, que la bouche délivre.[52]

The medieval religious frame underlines the naive joy of fruit, sun, clover, flower that convey erotic freshness. The gloria thereby "separates" the current of suffering that, at the end of *Lettera amorosa*, finds a corresponding equipoise in a different mode. After the thirty-six intervening paragraphs, almost all of which are brief, these last lines recapitulate the transmutation.

[50] "And the pain that comes from elsewhere / Finds at last its separation / In the flesh of our unity" ("A ***," *Commune Présence*, pp. 127-128).

[51] "Sharpener of my pain I suffer . . ." ("Lettera amorosa," *Commune Présence*, p. 142).

[52] "Hailing Love, the Beloved will come, / Gloria of summer, Oh fruit! / The sun's arrow will cross her lips, / Naked clover will curl on her flesh, / Miniature like the iris, the orchid, / The prairie's oldest gift to pleasure / Instilled by the cascade, freed by the mouth" (*ibid.*, p. 137).

Merci d'être, sans jamais te casser, iris, ma fleur de gravité. Tu élèves au bord des eaux des affections miraculeuses, tu ne pèses pas sur les mourants que tu veilles, tu éteins des plaies sur lesquelles le temps n'a pas d'action, tu ne conduis pas à une maison consternante, tu permets que toutes les fenêtres reflétées ne fassent qu'un seul visage de passion, tu accompagnes le retour du jour sur les vertes avenues libres.[53]

The thanksgiving offers a long sequence of open e sounds that establish a strong line of continuity, rhythmic balance, internal assonance. All receives shape and contour, however, from the liturgical enumeration that transforms the beloved into a figure of worship. There is also, more subtly, a systole and diastole of language, a mystical rhetoric. The opening words establish the duality of being ("être") as not non-being ("sans jamais te casser . . . "), and this is taken up in the succeeding parallelisms: enshrined affection is described as not oppression, consolation as not desolation, remedy as not bane, passionate union as not confinement. Char thereby weaves a paradoxical texture; he states and qualifies, denies and declares. Just as his parallelisms are liturgical, so is his theme, which proposes the portrait of a woman of miraculous affection and timeless healing. Yet merely to affirm this would be to offer oneself to the barbs of irony, whereas to affirm and negate is to compose the body spiritual, the "space" and "freedom" of a love that is both immanent and transcendent, absent and present, sought after and seeking. By means of an art founded in the rhetoric of religion *Lettera amorosa* projects the poet's generosity in the midst of loneliness and spells

[53] "Thank you for being, without ever breaking, iris, my flower of gravity. You raise on the water's edge miraculous affections, you do not weigh on the dying whom you attend, you heal wounds on which time has no effect, you do not lead to a troublesome house, you allow all the reflected windows to make a single countenance of passion, you accompany daylight's return on the green avenues of freedom" (*ibid.*, p. 143).

out, after "Le Visage nuptial," the grace which he elsewhere proposes in terms of the hunter wounded for beauty's sake yet unfaltering in pursuit:

> Celui qui marche sur la terre n'a rien à redouter de l'épine, dans les lieux finis ou hostiles. Mais s'il s'arrête et se recueille, malheur à lui! Blessé au vif, il vole en cendres, archer repris par la beauté.[54]

"Mais s'il s'arrête et se recueille . . . ": I have emphasized Char's moral and artistic metamorphosis which occurred around his thirtieth year. Its extent makes us think of Mallarmé, or Yeats: in each such case there was flight from asphyxia and brutal self-assertion. "Aux uns la prison et la mort," Char wrote in 1938, "aux autres la transhumance du Verbe."[55] This change was associated in his work with a return to nature and a reappraisal of love, but it also directly involved his practice as a poet. He found himself frequenting no longer the small circle of faithful around Breton and, instead, enunciating the equipollent necessity of dream and lucidity, "devil's nightingale" and "angel's key." As welcome as daylight, another clarity appears: "Sur les arêtes de notre amertume, l'aurore de la conscience s'avance et dépose son limon."[56]

A poetic statement of this attitude came early, in 1935, with the poem "Commune Présence." Its composition was preceded by many others in which art was itself the subject of poetry, including "Artine" and some of the earliest texts, the lyricism of which rings true although the later manner is many times more exigent. However, another

---

[54] "He who walks the earth has nothing to fear from the thorn, in finite or hostile places. But if he stops to meditate, woe unto him! Stung to the quick, he flies to ashes, bowman recaptured by beauty" ("Front de la rose," *Commune Présence*, p. 112).

[55] "For some, prison and death, for others the migration of the Word" ("Argument," *Fureur et Mystère*, Gallimard, 1967, p. 19).

[56] "On the ridges of our bitterness, the aurora of consciousness advances and lays its silt" (*ibid.*).

page written during his Surrealist years speaks with particular density. It offers the ambiguous meeting of will and imagination: "Je me voulais *événement*. Je m'imaginais *partition*."[57] Here is the pathetic transition of apple into skull; at the same time, the poet willfully decides to give the name of apple to his hallucination, which leads him to comprehend through word play that the "pomme," or skull/apple, is a "poème." We have thus an allegory of the creative act that calls on the resources of sentiment and fantasy, obsession and expression; it is an admirable example of Surrealist prose in its terse brevity. Nevertheless it contains an egocentrism that we saw to have been channeled and transcended in poems such as "Les poings serrés . . . " and "Le Visage nuptial." In "Commune Présence" likewise, Char traces a consciously willed change that on this occasion is carried out in the name, not of nature or love, but of poetry itself. Thus, between "Je me voulais événement" and this other text, a compulsion has been found to forge an art that communicates with its audience, that is linked to the springs of life, that embodies struggle, sacrifice, fervent union with the ideal. As he has written: "Comment me vint l'écriture? Comme un duvet d'oiseau sur ma vitre, en hiver. Aussitôt s'éleva dans l'âtre une bataille de tisons qui n'a pas encore à présent, pris fin."[58] Char knew he must henceforth endlessly explore whole virginal areas of winter landscape and fire, rigor and fertility.

[57] "I willed myself *event*. I imagined myself *musical score*" ("Je me voulais événement," *Commune Présence*, p. 195). The ambiguity of the Surrealist poet's mode of being is expressed with parallel urgency in "L'Instituteur révoqué" (*L'Action de la justice est éteinte*, p. 31) in which Char speaks of "le champ de dix hectares dont je suis le laboureur, le sang secret et la pierre catastrophique" ("the ten-hectare field of which I am the ploughman, the secret blood and the catastrophic stone").

[58] "How did writing come to me? Like a bird's down on my windowpane, in winter. Immediately in the hearth a battle of embers broke out that has not yet, even now, come to an end" ("La Bibliothèque est en feu," *Commune Présence*, p. 211.).

The first version of "Commune Présence" published in
Moulin premier is twenty lines longer than the poem as it
appears in subsequent collections. Later omitted, the introduction is reflective and stationary, whereas the second
part advances with urgency, addresses the reader in the
second person singular. The use of free verse is not exceptional in the early work, but in these lines it is imbued with
solar virility, the development of which comprises three
sections—the first two of almost exactly equal length (lines
one to thirteen, lines fourteen to twenty-five), the third of
two lines only. It is clear from the start that a huge impa-
tience reigns:

Tu es pressé d'écrire
Comme si tu étais en retard sur la vie.
S'il en est ainsi fais cortège à tes sources.
Hâte-toi.
Hâte-toi de transmettre
Ta part de merveilleux de rébellion de bienfaisance.
Effectivement tu es en retard sur la vie,
La vie inexprimable,
La seule en fin de compte à laquelle tu acceptes de t'unir,
Celle qui t'est refusée chaque jour par les êtres et par les
    choses,
Dont tu obtiens péniblement de-ci de-là quelques
    fragments décharnés
Au bout de combats sans merci.
Hors d'elle, tout n'est qu'agonie soumise, fin
    grossière.[59]

[59] "You are in a hurry to write / As if you were lagging behind life. / If
this is so, fall in behind your sources. / Hurry / Hurry to transmit / Your
share of marvel rebellion beneficence. / In truth you are lagging behind
life, / Inexpressible life, / The only life you finally agree to wed, / The one
you are refused each day by beings and things, / From which you labori-
ously obtain here and there a few gaunt fragments / At the conclusion of
merciless struggles. / Everything outside it is merely submissive agony,
vulgar end."

The lines move by their combined haste, mystery, clarity. The repetitions, the military metaphors, the underlying notion of sexual desire convey a radical energy that must perforce find expression. They go together with a muscular energy that takes as its basic rhythm the hexasyllable and, as its keynote, the strident continuity of assonantal i—"écrire," "vie" (three times), "si," "ainsi," "inexprimable," "t'unir," "merci," "agonie soumise." Yet, alongside this phonetic drive, there is the lucidly articulated mystery of that which is sought after and not obtained, yet nonetheless fragmentarily grasped. It makes us think of Surrealist ambitions: "le merveilleux" might well come straight from a Breton text, as could "la rébellion" and "la bienfaisance," if it were not for the generality with which Char conveys his urge to speak to his fellow-men. An allegorical intent is implicit, which the poet himself annotates by a personal declaration included in *Partage formel* of 1942: " . . . voici que l'obscurité s'écarte et que VIVRE devient, sous la forme d'un âpre ascétisme allégorique, la conquête des pouvoirs extraordinaires dont nous nous sentons profusément traversés mais que nous n'exprimons qu'incomplètement faute de loyauté, de discernement cruel et de persévérance."[60] To write is to dedicate oneself to an idea of life as jealous as that of Rimbaud, as magisterial as his command to "change life."

In the second section the poet envisages his own death and the demolition of present dwelling-places (here, too, we recall Rimbaud's words: "En tout cas, rien des apparences actuelles"; again: "Il y a des destructions nécessaires").[61]

---

[60] " . . . now darkness moves aside and LIVING becomes, in the form of a harsh allegorical asceticism, the conquest of the extraordinary powers we feel coursing abundantly in us but which we only express incompletely for lack of loyalty, cruel discernment, perseverance" (*Poèmes et Prose choisis*, p. 220).

[61] "In any case, nothing of present appearances;" "There are necessary destructions."

Si tu rencontres la mort durant ton labeur,
Reçois-la comme la nuque en sueur trouve bon le
    mouchoir aride,
En t'inclinant.
Si tu veux rire,
Offre ta soumission,
Jamais tes armes.
Tu as été créé pour des moments peu communs.
Modifie-toi, disparais sans regret
Au gré de la rigueur suave.
Quartier suivant quartier la liquidation du monde se
    poursuit
Sans interruption,
Sans égarement.[62]

Affirmations alternate with conditionals and imperatives
as death is accepted sensuously, but not defeat. Rigorous
and suave after the fashion of poetry itself, a fatal law de-
crees the change, accomplishes the purge. No less than
total sacrifice is required: self and city will yield to ceaseless
onslaught as images of war, short verses, frequent end-
stopping (there are five periods in the section) translate the
poet's readiness to destroy or be destroyed.

Essaime la poussière.
Nul ne décèlera votre union.[63]

The coda promises that the goal will be reached, inter-
course achieved like that of the child-poet Rimbaud with
the dawn. The two verbs "essaime" and "décèlera" are determined phonologically by the previous text; they suggest

[62] "If you meet death during your toil, / Receive it as the sweating neck
welcomes the dry handkerchief / With head bent forward. / If you want to
laugh, / Offer your submission, / Never your weapons. / You were created
for uncommon moments. / Change, disappear without regret / At the will
of smooth severity. / District after district the world continues to be liq-
uidated / Without interruption, / Without aberration."
[63] "Let the dust swarm. / No one will discover your union."

the sweetness of honey, the golden dust of union, the mystery of this consummation. Although the name is not uttered, we have again the myth of Orion, the pattern of hunt and hunter, the meeting of violence and love. The poet lives by the paradox of expressing the inexpressible, capturing the intrinsically elusive, of which "Commune Présence" provides an early statement. There is, however, no escape from anguish but resilience—more, happiness in the face of tragic odds. As Char has written: "L'acte poignant et si grave d'écrire quand l'angoisse se soulève sur un coude pour observer et que notre bonheur s'engage nu dans le vent du chemin."[64]

Following the internal drama of "Je me voulais événement" and the dynamism of "Commune Présence," we think of any number of poems in which the new art is explicitly pursued. Henceforth Char considers the Surrealists to be "incapables de toiser l'universalité du drame,"[65] powerless before the Spanish Civil War and the atrocities of Hitlerism; instead, his experience of the maquis confirms, and deepens, his practice of a conscious art. Much recalls Malraux, much also Camus in this revaluation, but neither expresses with a warmth comparable to Char's the role of art in an age of torture. Thus, in the beautiful "Débris mortels et Mozart," it is no longer the self-regarding poet of the early writings who speaks but the poet-critic of Georges Braque, Miró, Ernst, Picasso, Giacometti, Brauner, de Staël, of others who voyage across "le splendide mutisme de la peinture";[66] of Rembrandt and Georges de la Tour; of the painters of Lascaux, as well as those of the New Hebrides and New Guinea. His pic-

[64] "The poignant and so grave act of writing when anguish rises on one elbow to observe, and happiness goes forth naked in the wind of the path" (*Recherche de la base et du sommet*, p. 162).

[65] "Unable to gauge the universality of the drama" ("Partage formel," *Poèmes et Prose choisis*, p. 220).

[66] "The resplendent muteness of painting" (*Recherche de la base et du sommet*, p. 75).

tural interests are broad, his tributes those of a man who exults in painting's conflict with the real. He has similarly been generous in hailing writers; has named predecessors who range from the troubadours to Reverdy; and, in particular, has written definitive remarks on the poet who, more than all others, is at the root of his writing: Rimbaud. Concerning Rimbaud, he has eloquently attested his exceptional affinity: "Mais si je savais ce qu'est Rimbaud pour moi, je saurais ce qu'est la poésie devant moi, et je n'aurais plus à l'écrire."[67] Indeed, we may take his work, in style, themes, and intent, to be the transvaluation— through and beyond Surrealism—of Rimbaud's, whereby the quest for love, science, violence in the *Illuminations* is pursued in conformity with a redemptional myth. But as we have already noted, music is not absent from the number of arts to which he turns: included in *La Parole en archipel* in 1963, "Débris mortels et Mozart" expresses art's victory over death. Its parts are arranged in the manner of a symphony that mimes a largo, an allegro, an adagio. No anecdote is latent, nor any argument, but three movements find an accord.

The first paragraph, a single sentence, is composed of seven sections, including one group of twenty syllables.

> Au petit jour, une seule fois, le vieux nuage rose dépeuplé survolera les yeux désormais distants, dans la majesté de la lenteur libre; puis ce sera le froid, l'immense occupant, puis le Temps qui n'a pas d'endroit.[68]

By rhythmic modulation Char translates the rising swell of a vision of familiar beauty, one last tender farewell, fol-

---

[67] "But if I knew what Rimbaud is for me, I should know what poetry lies ahead of me, and I should no longer have to write it" (*ibid.*, p. 102).

[68] "Before dawn, one single time, the old pink untenanted cloud will soar above the eyes henceforth distant, in the majesty of free deliberation; then there will be cold, the vast occupant, then Time that has no place" ("Débris mortels et Mozart," *Commune Présence*, p. 206).

lowed by the cold vastness of death. The future tense announces an end, and the adverbs and adverbial phrases, through their ternary progression, emphasize the fatal inevitability of the language.

The second part is of a different kind. It offers a relatively short protasis and a long apodosis corresponding to an accent that denies despair.

> Sur la longueur de ses deux lèvres, en terre commune, soudain l'allégro, défi de ce rebut sacré, perce et reflue vers les vivants, vers la totalité des hommes et des femmes en deuil de patrie intérieure qui, errant pour n'être pas semblables, vont à travers Mozart s'éprouver en secret.[69]

Here, in a complex paragraph, the octosyllabic measure is heard four times and provides the continuo. On this foundation two groups of five syllables, one of twenty-one, an alexandrine, work their changes, construct their consolation. A proudly human art speaks from beyond death to whosoever seeks the lost country and the reintegrated self. After the deliberateness of the first paragraph, these lines eschew solitude for living men and women in the gracious allegro, undying music and familiar exchange, suggested by the phrase "à travers Mozart."

Having countered death by a living art, the poem concludes on a note of virile lyricism.

> —Bien-aimée, lorsque tu rèves à haute voix, et d'aventure prononces mon nom, tendre vainqueur de nos frayeurs conjuguées, de mon décri solitaire, la nuit est claire à traverser.[70]

[69] "Suddenly, on the length of its two lips, in the common earth, the allegro, the challenge of this sacred rejection, pierces and flows back toward the living, the whole mass of men and women mourning for the inner country who, wandering so as not to be alike, will secretly test themselves through Mozart."

[70] " 'Beloved, when you dream aloud, and perchance pronounce my name, tender vanquisher of our conjoined fears, of my solitary objurgation, the night is bright to cross.' "

Once again we find an octosyllabic measure that occurs twice; there is, however, no long phrase as in the first two parts, but the shorter rhythms of an adagio. A voice whispers to the beloved, pronounces the exorcism that Mozart achieves and that, on another level, lovers instinctively find for themselves. Fear is banished, vexation calmed, darkness illuminated: structure and theme compose the pattern of redemption that, above any hedonistic role, is art's function, as it is that of its analogues, love and nature; and where "Je me voulais événement" spoke for one man, "Débris mortels et Mozart" affirms freedom for all.

More recent poems on the theme of art would repay close analysis, but I shall refer to one short piece only, published in *Dans la pluie giboyeuse* of 1968. Its scientific title notwithstanding, "Dyne" offers a unit, not of physics, but of artistic force. It comprises two paragraphs of almost identical length, although the first moves strongly to a climax within the span of a single sentence, and the second is divided into four periods that affirm, exclaim, formulate a rhetorical question in a manner both abstract and didactic:

> Passant l'homme extensible et l'homme transpercé, j'arrivai devant la porte de toutes les allégresses, celle du Verbe descellé de ses restes mortels, faisant du neuf, du feu avec la vérité, et fort de ma verte créance je frappai.[71]

Char first gives the narrative of personal experience, the lyrical account of a journey beyond the potential and the pathetic. The past definite tense is that of a joyful initiation—the same as that by which the poem is won against death: the artist believes in a burning truth which for him is the ultimate end and beginning of happiness.

---

[71] "Going beyond extensible man and man transpierced, I reached the door of all happiness, that of the Word unsealed of its mortal remains, making newness, fire with truth, and strong by virtue of my verdant belief I knocked" (*Le Nu perdu*, Gallimard, 1971, p. 78).

Built with discreet elegance on the equilibrium of two
alexandrines in the first and last phrases, the sentence espouses the progression of a spiritual odyssey.

Now, however, the technique changes as narrative becomes promise, first person singular gives way to second,
short analytical phrases replace the lyrical swell:

> Ainsi atteindras-tu au pays lavé et désert de ton
> défi. Jusque-là, sans calendrier, tu l'édifieras. Sévère
> vanité! Mais qui eût parié et opté pour toi, des sites
> immémoriaux à la lyre fugitive du père?[72]

To whom are the words of reassurance addressed? To the
self, but also to all who, working to fulfil a dream, devote
themselves to a selfless task. The poet, the artist, discovers
his ancestral calling in ageless myth and familiar heritage.
Nothing would seem to have designated him and yet he
achieves his necessity in making a time without calendar, a
country without blemish, which flood and solitude have
purified. An essential bearing has been taken, and the energy, or salutary dyne, suffuses imagination and will.

This short prose-poem was written in a period of restraint as severe as the wall at the source of the stream. Yet
"Dyne" is in harmony with the three previous poems in
that it likewise expresses the paradox of the fluent and the
lapidary, both the impulsiveness of "Commune Présence"
and the smiling emancipation—"porte de toutes les
allégresses"—of "Je me voulais événement" and "Débris
mortels et Mozart." Nevertheless, these four modulations
on the theme of art offer but a glimpse of Char's dialectic.
Central in this regard are his aphorisms, often as dense as
whole poems, among which one may recall: "La poésie
est, de toutes les eaux claires, celle qui s'attarde le moins

---

[72] "Thus shall you reach the washed and empty country of your challenge. Until then, without a calendar, you will build it. Unsparing vanity!
But who would have wagered and chosen you, from sites immemorial to
the father's fugitive lyre!"

au reflet de ses ponts,"[73] which provides the image of limpidity, force, desire, openness to the future, movement, the extreme contrary of solipsism; or this best known of his formulations: "Le poème est l'amour réalisé du désir demeuré désir,"[74] wherein is spelt out the endless exchange of love and lover, hunt and hunter, sexual passion consummated yet undiminished, the dénouement that remains constant tension and is the poem's field of force; or this more recent one, of special resonance, which appeared in *La Nuit talismanique*: "Faire la brèche et qu'en jaillisse la flambée d'une fleur aromatique."[75] The poem envisaged is as compact as stone, opaque yet splendid; rockface breached by lightning; wall encountering prairie; the union of closed substance and evanescent aroma. We could not wish for words that more succinctly project the poetics of violence and grace.

It will be evident from the foregoing remarks that neither *Aromates chasseurs* nor Char's other mature work separates nature, or love, or art, from philosophy. From the age of thirty an incandescent reason presides—"une exigence de la conscience . . . à laquelle nous ne pouvons nous soustraire."[76] Poetry is responsible language that flees narrow limits in order to articulate the hostility of beauty to death. The urgent need is for clarity of moral purpose, which one cannot but contrast with the attitude contained in Surrealist pieces such as "Les Asciens" (the title is a neologism designating those who choose not to know) in which we read: "Nous apparaissons comme les végétaux complets /

[73] "Of all clear waters, poetry tarries least in the reflection of its bridges" ("A la santé du serpent," *Poèmes et Prose choisis*, p. 94).

[74] "The poem is the consummated love of desire that remains desire" ("Partage formel," *Poèmes et Prose choisis*, p. 223).

[75] "Make the breach, and let there burst forth the flame of an aromatic flower" (*La Nuit talismanique*, Geneva, Skira, Collection "Les Sentiers de la création," 1972, p. 67).

[76] "A demand for consciousness . . . from which we cannot escape" (*Recherche de la base et du sommet*, p. 8).

Envahisseurs du nouvel âge primitif."[77] The mature poet, on the contrary, seeks to be the most consciously human he is capable of, to consider his act in relation to all acts, to multiply his concern. As he writes: "Je m'inquiète de ce qui s'accomplit sur cette terre, dans la paresse de ses nuits, sous son soleil que nous avons délaissé"; again: "Rien ne m'obsède que la vie."[78]

The family of thinkers to whom he belongs is not hard to define, and he makes no secret of it. He finds himself with Heraclitus, whose aphorisms have in his own a noble accompaniment; with Nietzsche, Lautréamont, Rimbaud; with the philosophers and poets of the antistatic. With reasoned fury he recognizes that we live in tragedy, our duty being to give a name to the absurd: "L'homme n'est qu'une fleur de l'air tenue par la terre, maudite par les astres, respirée par la mort . . . "; "Nous sommes ce jour plus près du sinistre que le tocsin lui-même. . . ."[79] The war brought daily awareness of this and might well have led, by lucidity, to despair; yet *Feuillets d'Hypnos* is a book of courage and dignity. In the heat of battle and the memory of outrage, values were whetted: "La perception du fatal," he writes, "la présence continue du risque, et cette part de l'obscur plongeant dans les eaux, tiennent l'heure en haleine et nous maintiennent disponibles à sa hauteur."[80] If pessimism is inevitable, an "illusion" remains, the mystery of happiness, tears, love, hope. As

---

[77] "We appear like complete plants / Invaders of the new primitive age" (*Le Marteau sans maître*, p. 52).

[78] "I worry about what is done on this earth, in the laziness of its nights, beneath its sun that we have abandoned"(*Recherche de la base et du sommet*, p. 13); "Nothing but life obsesses me" ("Le Météore du 13 août," *Fureur et Mystère*, p. 203).

[79] "Man is but a flower of the air held by the earth, cursed by the stars, inhaled by death . . ." ("A une sérénité crispée," *Poèmes et Prose choisis*, p. 249); "We are this day closer to disaster than the tocsin itself" ("Les Compagnons dans le jardin," *ibid.*, p. 281).

[80] "The perception of fatality, the continuous presence of risk, and that part of darkness plunging in the waters, hold the hour breathless and keep us ready on its peak" (*Recherche de la base et du sommet*, p. 117).

close as the heart and as inexplicable, a passionate gainsaying of death distinguishes the language of poetry from any other: "A chaque effondrement de preuves le poète répond par une salve d'avenir."[81] This, as we know, is the sense of the tragic hero stricken by the gods, who yet rises and goes beyond. On the logic of Orion's desperate optimism, the poem constitutes a form as penetrable and defiant as field and rock. I shall refer in the following pages to four poems that state the poet's anguish and, at the same time, recapitulate the themes in the light of a compelling awareness.

Among the writings that date from the war, "Le Bouge de l'historien" is especially worthy of note in that it views those years in terms of an intimate confession—"l'hallucinante expérience de l'homme noué au Mal."[82] Its opening is a contained cry of anguish: "La pyramide des martyrs obsède la terre";[83] but hieratic suffering writes in starkest image what the historian of himself sees as past irresoluteness. In Surrealism he has already known the empire of unreason rampant, of sensibility divorced from sense:

> Onze hivers tu auras renoncé au quantième de l'espérance, à la respiration de ton fer rouge, en d'atroces performances psychiques. Comète tuée net, tu auras barré sanglant la nuit de ton époque. Interdiction de croire tienne cette page d'où tu prenais élan pour te soustraire à la géante torpeur d'épine du Monstre, à son contentieux de massacreurs.[84]

[81] "For every collapse of proofs the poet responds with a salvo from the future" ("Partage formel," *Poèmes et Prose choisis*, p. 227).

[82] "The hallucinating experience of man bound fast to Evil."

[83] "The pyramid of martyrs obsesses the earth" (*Poèmes et Prose choisis*, p. 25).

[84] "For eleven winters you will have renounced the rendezvous of hope, the respiration of your red-hot iron, in terrible psychic performances. A comet killed outright, you will have barred with blood the night of your time. You are forbidden from believing that page to be your own which you used to escape the giant torpor of the Monster's thorn, its wrangling butchers."

The words become a means of reckoning as the "tu" form distances and thereby indicts the self, and the future perfect tense describes an overdue completion. Char numbers his years of ungoverned night, of ownerless hammer, when will was rejected for psychic performance, when his best efforts to deny the specter of torpor were not wholly accountable: "Interdiction de croire tienne cette page. . . ." His poetic venture of the 'thirties is castigated in words that take stock of a burden unassumed. Now he gives vent to his pent-up disgust:

> Miroir de la murène! Miroir du vomito! Purin d'un feu plat tendu par l'ennemi![85]

Shark, vomit, manure, fire—not the fire that leaps but one that smoulders and palls—the presence of the enemy: Char criticizes not Surrealism itself, but a gutless acceptance of horror, a renunciation that in turn he renounces with loathing. His words break the chains of self-satisfaction. Yet the last lines of the poem go beyond this spleen and express the verdant hope that has been absent too long:

> Dure, afin de pouvoir encore mieux aimer un jour ce que tes mains d'autrefois n'avaient fait qu'effleurer sous l'olivier trop jeune.[86]

Evil is not wholly exorcized, nor resolution reached, but Char formulates a rule by which he may live, that is both injunction and active faith. The remembered ideal must be found again, loved more deeply. Conveyed by way of the image of the olive-tree, it restores the sensuous bond with nature, the associations with Mediterranean warmth, which are placed alongside the nightmare. History has

[85] "Shark's mirror! Mirror of vomit! Manure of flat fire held by the enemy!"

[86] "Endure, so one day you can love still better that which your former hands only touched beneath the too young olive-tree."

broken into an indulgent world and shown that the poem must be a moral act, a total commitment to poetry and truth, agile bird and deliberate tree. "L'oiseau et l'arbre," he writes, "sont conjoints en nous. L'un va, l'autre maugrée et pousse."[87]

Another piece from the same series of "Neuf Poèmes pour vaincre" published in 1945, "Hommage et famine" has as its focus no longer redeeming nature, but the presence of the woman. The title is a play on words since it echoes "homme" and "femme," the image of the couple as contemplated in the midst of war kindling amorous tribute, stirring erotic appetence, revealing the multiple lesson of love. The first long paragraph comprises two sentences of almost equal length:

> Femme qui vous accordez avec la bouche du poète, ce torrent au limon serein, qui lui avez appris, alors qu'il n'était encore qu'une graine captive de loup anxieux, la tendresse des hauts murs polis par votre nom (hectares de Paris, entrailles de beauté, mon feu monte sous vos robes de fugue). Femme qui dormez dans le pollen des fleurs, déposez sur son orgueil votre givre de médium illimité, afin qu'il demeure jusqu'à l'heure de la bruyère d'ossements l'homme qui pour mieux vous adorer reculait indéfiniment en vous la diane de sa naissance, le poing de sa douleur, l'horizon de sa victoire.[88]

[87] "The bird and tree are united in us. One sallies, the other grumbles and strives" (*Recherche de la base et du sommet*, p. 163).

[88] "Woman attuned to the poet's mouth, this serene-silted torrent, who taught him when he was still only a captive seed of anxious wolf the tenderness of the tall walls polished by your name (acres of Paris, entrails of beauty, my fire rises beneath your dresses of flight). Woman asleep in the pollen of flowers, place on his pride your hoar-frost of limitless medium, so that until the hour of the heather of bones he remains the man who the better to adore you thrust back indeterminately in you the reveille of his birth, the fist of his pain, the horizon of his victory" (*Poèmes et Prose choisis*, p. 27).

We find two parallel curves that resume the past, summon the future. The first, with no main verb, details a harmony that speaks with the voice of the poet—matutinal, tumultuous—but also calm and bearing its gravity like a body of silt with unhurried speed. The poet evokes the wall of tenderness that guided his anxiety, names in the first person the city he identifies with the woman, his desire for her that cannot be satisfied. Proceeding in eight rhythmic groups of varied length, the period discovers the hexasyllabic measure that occurs here three times (it occurs three further times in the rest of the text), and serves thereby as the basic element of regularity; we are also sensitive to the power of alliteration and assonance. Yet the second invocation is no less fervent and musical: like the opening, it begins on a sensual image; however, it quickly modulates into a prayer addressed to the woman's magical power so that all the future, until the hour of death, may be protected. The poet would wish her to be, as before, inseparable from his exultant birth, his defiant pain, his constant expectation. The images of nature take on a special force, for prairie answers wall, "la tendresse des hauts murs" of the first sentence asserting a vital complementarity. Divided into five sections, the rhythm includes a sequence of forty-five syllables that traces out the giant parabola of adoration.

In the second paragraph the rhythms are staccato, the sentences—of which there are four—comparatively short, the tenses varied—past definite, imperfect, pluperfect.

(Il faisait nuit. Nous nous étions serrés sous le grand chêne de larmes. Le grillon chanta. Comment savait-il, solitaire, que la terre n'allait pas mourir, que nous, les enfants sans clarté, allions bientôt parler?)[89]

---

[89] "(It was night, We had held each other fast under the great oak of tears. The cricket chirped. How did he know in his solitude that earth was not about to die, that we children without light were soon going to speak?)"

The parentheses recall their use at the end of the first sentence like a rhyme for the eye. But they are also once more the occasion for the poet to speak in the first person, to express the intimate urgency that inspires the grandeur of his parallelisms. The first sentences allude to a precise moment of tenderness and pathos, which the cricket's cry interrupts. But instead of description, the last words form a question uttered with hindsight: the cricket announced life, and life there would be; the poet's words give the lie to sadness, affirm the facts as he knows them, for earth was not to die, night was to end, silence was to be broken. By a series of simple contrasts between life and death, darkness and light, infancy and speech, by echoes, homophones, isometry, witness is borne to future hope through the evidence of past good fortune. Thus, in the throes of war, Char writes a thanksgiving and a prayer, both devotion and entreaty, that is not reducible to a personal document but the fable of all whose victory—act, image, thought— lies before them.

Written after "Hommage et famine" and subsequent to the Liberation, "Madeleine à la veilleuse" appeared for the first time in the *Mercure de France* of July 1948. It is unique among Char's poems in that a later commentary published in *Recherche de la base et du sommet* relates an exceptional circumstance that attended its completion.[90] Char vouches for the truth of an event ("Je jure que tout ceci est vrai et m'est arrivé. . . .")[91] which he describes in detail: his chance meeting in the Paris underground the day he finished his poem with a young woman called Madeleine; a few intense verbal exchanges ("Restez accueillant," she says, "vous ne vous verrez pas mourir");[92] a short walk together in the dark streets and the same feeling of deep solitude and total favor as he had experienced earlier that day

[90] *Recherche de la base et du sommet*, pp. 47-50.
[91] "I swear that all this is true and happened to me. . . ."
[92] "Stay welcoming, you will not see yourself die."

on finishing his poem; finally, the woman's leave-taking
("Embrassez-moi, que je parte heureuse . . . ")[93] and disappearance into the metro. The encounter recalls the magical apparitions portrayed by the Surrealists, but Char gives
his account with personal sobriety, offers precise details,
proposes also a remark of a general nature: "L'accès d'une
couche profonde d'émotion et de vision est propice au sur-
gissement du grand réel."[94] There is, then, he postulates, a
layer from which the poem speaks and which is that of our
oracles and signs. However, in characteristic fashion, he
does not end his narration as if it were an isolated and ex-
otic experience for the happy few, but draws a lesson: "La
réalité noble ne se dérobe pas à qui la rencontre pour l'es-
timer et non pour l'insulter ou la faire prisonnière. Là est
l'unique condition que nous ne sommes pas toujours assez
purs pour remplir."[95] He declares his faith, his conviction
with respect to the virtues of courtesy, deference and
honor that we owe the preternatural.

This page explains the private aura, the dramatic
warmth the poem possesses for Char: it "proves" the constant significance of art. For "Madeleine à la veilleuse," his
inspiration was the painting of the same title by Georges de
la Tour, who has nourished many of his meditations and
whose "Prisonnier," in the form of a reproduction, hung
on the wall of his command-post during the maquis. In the
single paragraph of this poem, he expresses the contemporary impact of La Tour, whose canvases speak to us and
to our future. The structure is simple in its two conditional
propositions—one positive, the other negative—that open
the meditation, the two futures that state an imminent violence, the final two futures that bring the solace of La

[93] "Kiss me, so I may leave happy."
[94] "Access to a deep layer of emotion and vision is propitious to the up-
surge of the truly real."
[95] "Noble reality does not flee from those who meet it with respect, and
not to insult or confine. That is the sole condition which we are not always pure enough to fulfil."

Tour's lamp—"les minutes de suif de la clarté," the "exemplaire fontainier de nos maux."[96]

> Je voudrais aujourd'hui que l'herbe fût blanche pour fouler l'évidence de vous voir souffrir: je ne regarderais pas sous votre main si jeune la forme dure, sans crépi de la mort.[97]

The two periods of almost identical length voice the single thought of a suffering hateful to see. (We think of the note in *Feuillets d'Hypnos*: "Les yeux seuls sont à peine capables de pousser un cri.")[98] Instead of an aesthetic response, Char goes to the heart of his subject which is the visible demonstration—"évidence," "forme"—of pain and death investing beauty, the naked skull beneath the woman's hand. The circumflex pattern of both periods rises to a feminine apogee, ends on a masculine, tracing the same stern contour.

> Un jour discrétionnaire, d'autres pourtant moins avides que moi, retireront votre chemise de toile, occuperont votre alcôve.[99]

The desire for snow, for the softness that would conceal suffering, is cruelly answered: "discrétionnaire," "retireront," "occuperont" indicate an aggression like that of a savage horde. The sentence is shorter, the inflection passing from masculine apogee to feminine perigee, yet the quadripartite construction recalls the two opening periods.

[96] "The tallow minutes of brightness" ("Feuillets d'Hypnos," *Poèmes et Prose choisis*, p. 56); "exemplary fountain-maker of our ills" ("Justesse de Georges de la Tour," *Le Nu perdu*, p. 74).

[97] "Today I would wish the grass to be white to tread the evidence of seeing you suffer: I would not look at death's harsh uncoated form beneath your hand so young" (*Poèmes et Prose choisis*, p. 98).

[98] "The eyes alone are barely capable of uttering a cry" ("Feuillets d'Hypnos," *Poèmes et Prose choisis*, p. 46).

[99] "One arbitrary day, others though less avid than I will take off your homespun shift, occupy your alcove."

Mais ils oublieront en partant de noyer la veilleuse et un peu d'huile se répandra par le poignard de la flamme sur l'impossible solution. [100]

With a decisiveness similar to the adversatives of a Mallarmé sonnet, the "mais" adduces a leap of the imagination. Arbitrary power cannot but commit a fatal error, disregard the lamp which, in the midst of violence, asserts the presence of grace. Death and suffering are not thereby appeased—the solution remains "impossible"—but hope has become as irrefutable as death itself.

So Char's anguish, and his tortured recognition of the absurd, have recourse to nature in "Le Bouge de l'historien," to love in "Hommage et famine," to art in "Madeleine à la veilleuse"; yet they also find a solution in self-qualifying lucidity. The last poem I wish to consider is one of Char's finest. "J'habite une douleur" first appeared in the review *Poésie 45* in October-November 1945 and was included the following year in *Le Poème pulvérisé*. Seven years later Char published a marginal commentary on all the pieces in the collection; he called it *Arrière-histoire du poème pulvérisé*—"lampe directive, rigoureuse et sereine parmi l'ensemble souvent convulsif," "exorcisme en ma propre faveur contre la trombe d'innommable qui devait nous engloutir et dont nous émergeons."[101] These are, then, poems that come from the anguish of war, occupation, and the immediate post-war period. But the central piece around which the others crystallize is "J'habite une douleur." Char's note is important for us: "J'étais à cet instant lourd de mille ans de poésie et de détresse antérieure. Il fallait que je l'exprime. J'ai pris ma tête comme on saisit

---

[100] "But they will forget to put out the lamp when they leave and a little oil will pour from the dagger of the flame on the impossible solution."

[101] "Guiding lamp, rigorous and serene, in the midst of the often convulsive group," "exorcism for myself against the unnamable whirlpool that was to engulf us and from which we are now emerging" (*Arrière-histoire du poème pulvérisé*, p. 14).

une motte de sel et je l'ai littéralement pulvérisée. . . . De cette illusion atroce est né 'J'habite une douleur,' plus quelque calme."[102] The anguish is clear, no less than the violent need for relief by which the poem is realized. And yet from tension a stringent discipline stands forth. The title denotes the clear-eyed awareness which, instead of submitting to fate, consciously inhabits it. Our attention is called to an encompassing pain; nonetheless, as part of the rule to be unraveled, the three opening sentences resume an intimate lesson in the second person singular.

> Ne laisse pas le soin de gouverner ton cœur à ces tendresses parentes de l'automne auquel elles empruntent sa placide allure et son affable agonie. L'œil est précoce à se plisser. La souffrance connaît peu de mots.[103]

The poet addresses himself and at the same time speaks to his readers, his tone warm, his language abstract. The injunction, however, is rigorous as he warns against a manner of self-indulgence that is careless of decline, complaisant toward death. Such a tolerant attitude is preached by many, but Char reminds us that the glance cannot remain detached nor can suffering be cajoled. The second and third sentences, with their lively rhythms, point up the irony contained in the phrases "placide allure" and "affable agonie":

[102] "I was at that moment heavy with a thousand years of poetry and previous distress. I had to express it. I took my head as one seizes a block of salt and I literally shattered it. . . . From that frightful illusion 'J'habite une douleur' was born, as well as some calm" (*ibid.*, p. 27).

[103] "Do not leave the care of managing your heart to those tendernesses akin to autumn, from which they take its placid ways and congenial agony. The eye is quick to narrow. Suffering knows few words." One thinks of the surprising precocity of "Prêt au dépouillement" of 1928 (*Les Cloches sur le cœur*, p. 11) in which Char's mature voice is already heard: "Par ce temps de soleil veule de douceur sans contrariété il est inacceptable que la distance soit telle" ("In this time of sunlight listlessly kind and mellow it is unacceptable that distance should be such as it is").

> Préfère te coucher sans fardeau: tu rêveras du
> lendemain et ton lit te sera léger. Tu rêveras que ta
> maison n'a plus de vitres. Tu es impatient de t'unir au
> vent, au vent qui parcourt une année en une nuit. [104]

Instead of forebearance, the poet opts for the rejection of
a troublous past and present. Images of lightness preside
as the future is envisaged with the fullness of desire. By
the action of dream, the barriers of gravity, space, time
disappear; the self and the wind are one. Sound pattern,
rhythms, repetitions, images convey a lyrical delight
diametrically opposed to the atmosphere of the first section. Yet the twice occurring "tu rêveras" reminds us that
imagination exists precariously.

> D'autres chanteront l'incorporation mélodieuse, les
> chairs qui ne personnifient plus que la sorcellerie du
> sablier. Tu condamneras la gratitude qui se répète.
> Plus tard, on t'identifiera à quelque géant désagrégé,
> seigneur de l'impossible. [105]

The last three sentences of the first paragraph refer to
the same project but designate the wilful refusals in which
the self must engage: the refusal to celebrate the harmonious substance and enclave of time that love, or art, or natural beauty may propose (for to be fascinated by the present
is to fail the beauty unseen); the refusal to allow spon-
taneity to grow commonplace or gratitude to become trivial
(for repetition can kill feelings as it does words); the refusal
to limit one's ambitions to the reasonable and the possible
(for our only worthy goals are those which by definition
are unreachable). In the last line the vision becomes oracu-

---

[104] "Prefer to go to bed unburdened: you will dream of the morrow
and your couch for you will be light. You will dream that your house no
longer has window-panes. You are impatient to wed the wind, the wind
that covers a year in a night."

[105] "Others will sing of melodious embodiment, of flesh personifying
nothing any more but an hourglass magic. You will condemn gratitude
that repeats itself. Later you will be identified with some disaggregated
giant, lord of the impossible."

lar as austerity takes on the pathetic dimensions of a god
from some classical Hades, a huge form half-submerged
like an archipelago or a constellation—Orion single yet
many, scattered yet distinct. But even here the grandeur is
ironic, for, seen through other eyes, it is the epitome of
folly.

Pourtant.

In the same way as "Madeleine à la veilleuse," the
poem turns on an adversative, here an isolated word
placed strategically at the center of the text after the nine
sentences of the first paragraph and the nine others to
come. Nevertheless there is no triumphant new register
but a pause that signifies consciousness of failure. The
tense changes, and simultaneously the whole trajectory.

> Tu n'as fait qu'augmenter le poids de ta nuit. Tu es
> retourné à la pêche aux murailles, à la canicule sans
> été. Tu es furieux contre ton amour au centre d'une
> entente qui s'affole.[106]

Lightness has resulted in heaviness, union with the
wind in ponderous deliberation and the dog-days of the
soul, love in anger. Couched in the perfect and present
tenses, the three statements are built with rising accent
and the excited alliteration of fricatives and dentals. They
come as a challenge to past prophecies and imaginations:
we are forced to evaluate the distance between ambition
and act, to gauge the frenzied contradictions that thwart
our deepest affections.

> Songe à la maison parfaite que tu ne verras jamais
> monter. A quand la récolte de l'abîme?[107]

[106] "However. // You have only increased the weight of your night. You
have returned to fishing for ramparts, to summerless dog-days. You rage
against your love in the midst of a giddy consonance."

[107] "Think of the perfect house that you will never see rising. When will
the abyss be reaped?"

Further ironies emphasize the discordance, not of will and reality, but—still more bitterly—of dream and accomplishment. The other dwelling-place the poet postulates, the ideal habitation that inspires his resoluteness, shall not be constructed; the imagined harvest shall not be wrenched from the abyss. This is the black humor by which his lucidity finds the future no less barren than present and past. However, at a point where the goal most cherished is in jeopardy, the pattern of ternary development is arrested so that we discover the binary combination of injunction and question: the sharp self-raillery will have its equal and opposite response in the next two sentences.

Mais tu as crevé les yeux du lion. Tu crois voir passer la beauté au-dessus des lavandes noires. . . .[108]

For the second time we have an explicit adversative. It introduces two sentences that answer metrically and emotionally, in inverse order, the preceding lines. Despite evidence to the contrary, all has not been in vain; there has been irrefutable achievement, experiential proof. The self has been the hunter who blinds the lion, the seer who descries beauty in darkling nature; he is the personal witness of exploits and intuitions, the possessor of a vision that cannot be ignored. The heroic model, together with the image of desire traversing the darkness whose summer perfume it retains, counterpoint the previous irony and are the matter of myth.

As a consequence of the rising movement, the poet discovers his own ascent:

Qu'est-ce qui t'a hissé, une fois encore, un peu plus haut, sans te convaincre?[109]

[108] "But you have put out the lion's eyes. You believe you see beauty passing over the black lavender. . . ."
[109] "What has raised you once more a little higher, without convincing you?"

A question is asked, but the answer is already contained in the rest of the poem. The propelling force is that of consciousness and resolve, irony and desire, which gradually, obliquely—"par le biais et non par le droit fil" as *Aromates chasseurs* has it[110]—discover in pain a resilience whereby a third space can be achieved. The self has commanded the interplay of attitudes as they reject immobility in an ascesis that has no end. Will, imagination, hope are for a time victorious, though sorely pressed; and the two tetrasyllabic groups that conclude the sentence project a deliberate restraint.

The wisdom of the poem is finally summed up in a formulation that reverts to the image of the house.

Il n'y a pas de siège pur.[111]

In this last irony the height is viewed as a peak that must continually be regained: the self cannot once and for all build its home immune to danger and safe from dogmatism. Passion does not cease to be essential, but no more so than lucid distance, exacting appraisal. As we read in *Feuillets d'Hypnos*: "Epouse et n'épouse pas ta maison"; again, thirty years later, in *Le Nu perdu*: "Méfiez-vous de moi comme je me méfie de moi, car je ne suis pas sans recul."[112] Char's soliloquy traces out the scheme of tough-minded desire checking tragedy as it checks glibness, and articulates a rigor vibrant with contradiction. We find the counterpoise, and the implicit definition by its contrary, of Surrealism's "unowned hammer." Fantasy is held at bay,

---

[110] "Ces conflits entre le désir et l'esprit qui sème la désolation, conflits d'où l'esprit sort vainqueur par le biais et non le droit fil" ('La Frontière en pointillé," *Aromates chasseurs*, p. 116). "These conflicts between desire and the mind that sows desolation, conflicts from which the mind emerges victorious on the bias and not with the grain."

[111] "There is no innocent seat."

[112] "Marry and do not marry your house" (*Poèmes et Prose choisis*, p. 40); "Be wary of me as I am wary of myself, for I am not without detachment" ("Cotes," *Le Nu perdu*, p. 64).

pathos assumed, as a moral commitment is written into the text itself and not the margins alone.

Thus we are able to follow the dialectical pattern wrought by the poet. From nature to abstract thought by way of love and art, from oracular statement to litany, symphonic orchestration, dramatic monologue, the rhythm of downfall and ascent is admirably varied. Yet if the forms change, the sense is constant. Ten or twenty years ago one might have said of his œuvre that it was a language in search of a myth; now, however, with *Aromates chasseurs*, the myth is denominated that lights the work, sustains its thrust. The figure of Orion recalls its Hellenic heritage; tells of tragic fall, mysterious purgation; evokes the fertile coupling ever renewed of hunt and hunter. I find a poetry that is never facile but scrupulously self-aware, and charged with an urgency that addresses our time.

The Poem

I have discussed the encounter, by way of the figure of Orion, of violence and temperance, severity and tenderness, that animate Char's personal myth. On the one hand there is Vaucluse closed by the mountain-face; on the other a large plain swept by the winds of Provence offering its crops, its herbs and streams, its sun-drawn creatures. We may, then, hardly be surprised that a plaquette named *La Paroi et la Prairie* represents an important stage in the poet's career. Published in 1952 when he was forty-five, the sequence is a brilliant statement of his imaginative scheme.[1]

A first reading may find little proof of a presiding order. The verse is both free and regular, the prose laconic and discursive, the motifs multiple. It would seem that, within the limits he sets himself, Char is indulging a taste for diversity. We recall, moreover, that several of the ten pieces appeared separately, and that, even after 1952, they did not always form an ensemble in the selections he edited. Nevertheless we come to understand that he has here given us a compact bestiary in the medieval tradition that is the emblem of Orion mortally wounded yet resurgent. If there is no narrative continuum, as, for example, in the *Bestiaire d'amour* of Richard de Fournival, a single attitude interpenetrates the whole. From death to love, from wisdom to instinctive élan, Char expresses his tireless quest for a code by which to live.

The book is constituted of two equal parts, the first five pieces devoted to Lascaux, the second to animals of South-

[1] *La Paroi et la Prairie*, Paris, GLM, 1952, 32 p., later collected in *La Parole en archipel*, Paris, Gallimard, 1962.

ern France. We have seen the poet's attachment to his native region, his intimate sympathy for beasts, fish, and
fowl, his sense of a kindred relationship with the "peuple
des prés." We can therefore readily understand his choice
of four *fascinants*—massive bull, fluent trout, witty serpent,
exultant lark.[2] What, however, of Lascaux? Char has told
us that he first visited the paleolithic caves some years after
writing his poems. The seed of inspiration came thus not *in
situ* but rather from photographs taken by his friend Christian Zervos as well as from text and reproductions in Henri
Breuil's monumental study of 1952. Char, like many
another, considered the superb Lascaux forms with an
immediate wonder, attended to a language from unre-
membered dark. The cave, with its main chamber, its two
principal galleries, and the Shaft of the Dead Man, had for-
tuitously been discovered in the summer of 1940 by three
youths, but it was only after the war that its fame grew.
Breuil's *Quatre Cents Siècles d'art pariétal* was published in
the second quarter of 1952 (the *achevé d'imprimer* shows
April 25) and no doubt came into Char's hands shortly
thereafter. What appears certain is that the Lascaux series
was composed quickly; only one of the manuscripts is
dated—"Les Cerfs noirs" bears the mention "22 octobre
1952"—but they manifestly represent a continuous period
of creation. Confident of his work, the poet gave them to
the review *Cahiers d'Art* where they appeared in volume 2
for 1952. At the same time, the publisher Guy Lévis Mano
was preparing the collective edition of *La Paroi et la Prairie*,
which came off the press in December. So, I think, we
gather something of the impact the paintings had on Char,
and of the haste with which he wrote. At a summit of his
creative life that was also the period of *Lettera amorosa*, he

[2] The title "Quatre Fascinants" was given to the prairie series when it
was first published in the *Cahiers du Sud* (1950), and maintained the following year for a small plaquette. It serves as a subtitle in *La Paroi et la
Prairie*.

meditated on an ice age that balances the warmth of Provence. He was the man of the caverns working from within the mystery that cannot be dissolved—the "duvet de nuit noire"[3]—but also the inhabitant of warm fields and open sky. It is from the meeting of these two spheres that *La Paroi et la Prairie* reaches a compelling density, and articulates a legend of desire, whose referents are not nature alone, but love, art, thought itself.

"The true meaning cannot be grasped by the imagination," writes André Leroi-Gourhan of one of the most obscure of the Lascaux paintings.[4] It is this scene that serves as motif in the first poem of the series. An epigram spells out the legendary encounter of hunter and beast wherein, despite the protests of a methodologist like Leroi-Gourhan and in the absence of any sure guide, Char expresses the truth of the poet himself.

HOMME-OISEAU MORT ET BISON MOURANT

Long corps qui eut l'enthousiasme exigeant,
A présent perpendiculaire à la Brute blessée.

O tué sans entrailles!
Tué par celle qui fut tout et, réconciliée, se meurt,
Lui, danseur d'abîme, esprit, toujours à naître,
Oiseau et fruit pervers des magies cruellement sauvé.[5]

---

[3] "Down of black night" ("Le Nu perdu," *Le Nu perdu*, p. 31).

[4] *Histoire de l'Art*, Encyclopédie de la Pléiade, Paris, Gallimard, 1961, p. 71.

[5] "*Bird-man Dead and Bison Dying*: Long body whose enthusiasm was exacting, / At present perpendicular to the wounded Brute. // O innardless slain! / Slain by her who was all, and who dies reconciled, / He, abyss-dancer, spirit, ever about to be born, / Bird and fruit perverse cruelly saved from magic" (*La Paroi et la Prairie*, p. 11). The working manuscripts of the five Lascaux poems are part of the Collection René Char—Yvonne Zervos of the Fonds Doucet (AE-IV-17/734). The two versions of "Homme-Oiseau mort et Bison mourant" show several variants.

The title is his own. The early explorers of Lascaux refer
to the "Well Scene" ("Scène du Puits") and underline the
exceptional interest of this human being in the animal cor-
tege; yet, of the three figures shown, Char has chosen to
depict only two: at Lascaux the triangular composition contains on the left side a rhinoceros turning its back and run-
ning away. It too is perhaps an actor in the drama; or is it
an emblem of the defeated clan? However that may be, the
poet excludes this detail in order to focus on the bison and
the man. In the painting the beast stands over the corpse in
naturalistic fashion, portrayed in black on a background of
yellow clay. Its belly is pierced by a lance the man has
thrown, the entrails are falling from its side, its upright tail
is divided into three tufts. As for the man, he is treated in a
wholly different mode, his form a black tracing only
alongside the masterly projection of mass and movement.
The stiff body is a simple rectangle, the arms two lines that
end in four-fingered hands, the sex a trait pointing toward
the bison; the legs and feet, at right angles to one another,
are similarly linear, with thighs and calves merely sug-

First version:
l.2: (Raide) A présent perpendiculaire à la (Bête) (sa lyre) Brute blessée
l.4: (Mais) Lui plus avant toujours à naître oiseau
l.5: Et fruit pervers des magies (mystérieusement) obscurément (léger)
    sauvé

Second version:
l.4: Lui, plus avant, toujours à naître,
l.5: Oiseau et fruit pervers des magies, obscurément sauvé

In the proofs of *La Paroi et la Prairie* (Fonds Doucet AE-IV-17/736) l.5 reads:
    Lui, esprit, plus avant, successif, découvert, ardent, toujours à naître

The final reading is given in pencil. No draft could more clearly show
poetic creation as an act of discovery. Char does not follow pre-
established forms or thoughts but finds them by approximations in ad-
vancing from image to symbol, from a first schematic outline to a complex
expression. A variant such as "sa lyre" in line 2 is interesting in that, although the explicit notion will be abandoned, man and beast are conceived as no less complementary than the poet, this Orion-Orpheus, and
his instrument: when both are silent, the poem or product of their reconciliation will remain.

gested. But the most provocative aspect of this image is no doubt the small head in the form of a straight-billed bird, the significance of which is underscored by a similarly schematic bird perched on a stick beside the body. Such, then, is the Lascaux image that, more than any other, has inspired multiple interpretations and been seen in meta-physical and physical terms. Char's own reading is characterized by respectful precision—more, by a finely discriminating regard—that bears witness to his pressing concern.

Here lyricism is eschewed for a language descriptive and moral. This is the point of convergence of body and enthusiasm, dance and spirit, fruit and perversity. Nevertheless action is past and there are no main verbs: details recall action but distance it by the use of two past definites and five past participles. Thus, when the poem begins, antagonism is already over: having met like extreme lovers in mortal confrontation, the two adversaries are beyond the turmoil of struggle. Man it was who sought to fight, pressed by an unreasoned desire to encompass an adversary stronger than himself, to come to terms—the most severe of all—with the object of his wonder. In a voice of authority Char evokes the attitude and indicates the act, names the former passion and present repose that take on hieratic necessity. After the combat there is this geometrical arrangement ("long," "perpendiculaire"), the exactness of which is also suggested in the balance of the two alliterative groups of line 2. The man is dead, the bison dying, but they have reached a physical and emotional poise. The subject of the poem is, thus, properly the catharsis of a tragic event perceived, a fatality comprehended.

The poet has in a sense already expressed the whole substance of his drama. Yet his poem is not finished, for he proceeds to enter into his vision by way of an invocation vibrant with commitment. Laconically his exclamation breaks in on the previous deliberateness so as to convey a death that is no death, disembowelment that is purification. The hunter has become his own lighter self, an airy body, which Char puts before us in an apostrophe of great density. Across the ages he speaks to a living man, a miraculous familiar. Using the participle of line 3 as a springboard, an urgent summons wells up as he again alludes to the past and depicts the present; but the first and last words offer a material description framing values—the imperatives of love—that fired past action and resolved it. "Celle qui fut tout" is the essential contender, an idol subsuming the world, a godhead demanding nothing less than all. Yet the conflict expressed in the rising movement of the first hemistich is answered in the second, the pattern being circumflex: passion no longer reigns, but reconciliation, and the beast's death is followed by a definitive accounting. Experienced to its extreme point, emotion opens onto an order regained, like that of the tragic hero who by suffering is redeemed.

In the tight economy of the poem the last two lines turn from the image of the beast to that of man. They reach new phonetic intensity with an expanded rhythm, five occurrences of the sharp vowel i, three half-vowels. We are also held by the plurivalent language that reveals the complexity of the central actor: where before he was motionless and unsubstantial, he is now gracious movement vanquishing the abyss; he who was body has become spirit; though dead, he is about to be born; he is the bird, however fragile, that conquers despair. This, for Char, is the meaning of the mask and the totem: lightness has the advantage; the bird-song of an intimate alliance between man and nature carries the day. Nor is this triumph gratuitous as presented in the poem, since we realize that it results from the vigor of the poem straining against its own vocabulary of death, against the past definites, the participles: indeed, the verbal texture shows that struggle is the condition of salvation. Tension is brought to a climax in the final words that concentrate the drama in little: perverseness is man's identity—evil and good, earthy and transcendent, mortal and spiritual—which by the efforts he is capable of and, in particular, by his wilful sacrifice (here the echo of "perpendiculaire" in "pervers" finds its full significance), accomplishes his release from the obscure powers of magic, or the mystery within him that would otherwise remain nameless. Written in the last two words, as it is implicit in the total structure, the paradoxical design of defeat overcome is realized.

As so frequently in Char's work, "Homme-Oiseau mort et Bison mourant" has the binary structure of two homologous curves and, as it were, of two micro-narratives with past and present clearly demarcated. The first section contains an observation that is direct, while the second develops a heightened vision. Yet, playing across this simple pattern, a grammatical arrangement in three groups of two lines each corresponds to the three surges of the meter. After an opening composed of verses of ten and fourteen syllables, a pentasyllable arrests our attention, lending emphasis to the exclamation; line 4, however, consisting of fourteen syllables, has a breadth parallel to line 2; similarly, the last section, of eleven and fourteen syllables respectively, contains the metrical alliance of asymmetry and symmetry. It is apparent that the rhythmical freedom and varied pauses are punctuated by a balance that is the recurring measure of plenitude.

The sound shows the strong activity of plosives and dentals. Typical are five short alliterative groups connoting nervous intensity ("corps qui . . . ," "présent perpendiculaire," "Brute blessée," "tué . . . entrailles . . . tué . . . tout," "danseur d'abîme . . . "). These we hear as so many instants of recognition that allow no amplification. The insistence of half-vowels in the last four lines has a similar dramatic force ("tué," "tué," "réconciliée," "lui," "fruit," "cruellement"): a stylistic trait not expressive in itself, it becomes by repetition eloquent of poetic urgency. No rhyme occurs, but the two typographically separate sections conclude on words of identical syntactic function and on the same vowel; and this link is reinforced by the epithets at the caesurae whose first and last syllables echo one another like a solemn correspondence.

The poem has a beauty distinct from that of Char's other writings. Concerning it we are led to speak of the feeling of "clear and burning presence" Georges Bataille found at Lascaux.[6] Its brevity is not lack but incisiveness; its tenderness, strength; its precision, the hard-won language of spiritual courage. We are given the emblem of a nobility forged in conflict wherein man rises higher than himself and nature is likewise enhanced. Of the diverse ways of dying, that one is worthy which achieves sacrifice in the image of birth or resurrection, its hero taking on the mythical grandeur of Orion who triumphs at the moment of his death.

On the right wall of the section of Lascaux that Breuil called the nave, there is a painting of exceptional delicacy. It represents a succession of five heads of stags painted above a small ridge. They raise their nostrils as if to sniff the air—as if, writes Bataille, "they were emerging from the waters of a river."[7] The outline, the attitudes, the grouping make for one of our most indelible impressions of Lascaux. It is not surprising that Char should have been moved by the same image and led to write "Les Cerfs noirs."

LES CERFS NOIRS
Les eaux parlaient à l'oreille du ciel.
Cerfs, vous avez franchi l'espace millénaire,

[6] Georges Bataille: *La Peinture préhistorique: Lascaux ou la naissance de l'art*, Geneva, Skira, 1955; also in English, under the title *Lascaux, or the Birth of Art*, Skira, p. 12.
[7] *Lascaux*, p. 106.

Des ténèbres du roc aux caresses de l'air.

Le chasseur qui vous pousse, le génie qui vous voit,
Que j'aime leur passion, de mon large rivage!
Et si j'avais leurs yeux, dans l'instant où j'espère?[8]

Of six lines, one—the first—is a decasyllable with the caesura after the fourth syllable. It discovers discreetly the hexasyllabic rhythm that marks the poem, the five subsequent alexandrines measuring with deliberate regularity an idyllic scene of pastoral calm. Despite the absence of a rhyme scheme, the sound composes within this metrical framework a harmony of rare persuasiveness: the last word "j'espère" is prepared by "cerfs," "millénaire," "air," as well as by the assonance of open e, s and p. Intrinsic to the phonetic structure an anagram of hope is proposed, which is the central theme.

The tone is at furthest remove from that of "Homme-Oiseau mort et Bison mourant." Arranged in two parts, it uses the metaphor of communication in the first three lines ("parlaient à l'oreille . . . ," "vous avez franchi," "des . . .

[8] "*The Black Stags*: The waters were whispering in heaven's ear. / Stags, you have traversed millennial space, / From rocky darkness to the caress of air. // The hunter driving you, the genius seeing you, / How I love their passion from my own wide shore! / And perhaps their eyes are mine in my moments of hope?" (*La Paroi et la Prairie*, p. 12). The original manuscript held in the Fonds Doucet is written on an envelope. It is entitled "Les cerfs noirs de Lascaux" and dated "22 oct. 52":

Des ténèbres du roc aux caresses de l'air,
Cerfs vous avez franchi l'espace millénaire;
(Le glacier des vieux temps, la forêt souveraine)
Lorsque les eaux parlaient à l'oreille du ciel.
Le chasseur qui vous pousse, le génie qui vous voit,
Que j'aime leur (grandeur) passion (sur) de mon large rivage (étroit)!
(Ah! que n'ai-je) Et si j'avais leurs yeux (à) dans l'instant (que) où
   j'espère

The draft captures the thought and images in a single movement. Later, however, Char broke the sequence of six alexandrines, reversing the order of the first three lines and choosing to begin on a quieter end-stopped decasyllable. At the same time he sacrificed the original third line ("Le glacier des vieux temps, la forêt souveraine") which lacked neither amplitude nor force.

aux . . . ''), bringing together divergent aspects of nature and time. The second half turns from the description of this varied exchange to the world of the hunter and the artist who are both characterized by their passions, whether for physical capture or visual possession. In this way there is a shading of the voice, a gradation of tone and language that clearly distinguishes the first and second sections. A modification leads from a note that is properly elegiac to one of heightened self-awareness.

Nostalgically, the opening words call up an age of lyricism. In their simplicity they introduce a continuum of height and depth, water and sky. Fragmentation has yielded to the murmur of love: *in illo tempore* nature was undivided, scientific discourse had not erected its compartments, each element was intimately attentive to each. Char evokes no one historical epoch but an ideal locus of his imagination.

Having set the scene, he addresses himself to the stags as emblems of the spatial and temporal unity of nature. The water and sky of the opening were humanized by tenderness but now a direct relationship is established between nature and the poet himself. He must invoke the stags, speak to them in the conversational past, proclaim their triumph over time by way of time, their combination of darkness, mystery, depth, solidity—which is their mode as paintings—and lightness, joy, their sensuous bounding into the fullness of freedom (for the animals of Lascaux leap up, apparently without ground beneath them). Thus art achieves, in the figures of the stags, a miraculous connexity of rock and air, magical image and idea.

Yet, in an ever-widening perspective, man too is projected into the scene. The stags are not alone but are viewed, coveted, driven by the hunter who will capture and kill them. His desire is a vital one—not merely the pleasure of the hunt but the necessity to survive. And beyond the scene of stags and hunter is the Lascaux artist

pursuing mythical details with the eyes of genius, seeing
and remaking his prey, transcribing nature into art. His
will is no less intense than the hunter's, no less possessive.
And, finally, this double-edged passion of hunter and artist, killer and preserver, is itself further contemplated and
embraced from the far shore of time by the eye of the
twentieth-century poet who finds anew the portrait of
man's skill and aspiration, his enduring passion. Char proclaims his love for the forces of desire, his words an act of
recognition that answers primitive man's exultant energy
across the ages.

Like several of his poems, "Les Cerfs noirs" ends on a
question that is the contrary of a conclusion. It extends
once more the temporal and spatial perspective, on this occasion by an hypothesis regarding the way the poet envisages the future. We have advanced from the nostalgia with
which he began: the contemplation of art, the pursuit of
the imagination, having led in line 5 to a statement of personal commitment, now induces self-knowledge, or rather
speculation about the self. A link is supposed (although no
firm bridge is built) between the Lascaux scene and the
poet's intimate hope, that most subtly lyrical of attitudes.
For hope, as he realizes, may be conceived in the fashion of
man as both hunter and artist, who turns towards the de-
sired object in order to grasp it but finds a sign, the inexhaustible substance of a goal forever ahead; hope is the
perennial dream of reconciliation—water and sky, darkness and light, stone and air, the grace that nature offers
and that art uniquely suggests, the unity we touch but
cannot have and hold. The poem expresses this and, at the
same time, beyond affirmation, traces out the elusive line
of flight that is its own trajectory.

We are reminded of certain poems by Char's contemporary, Jules Supervielle: "Les Cerfs noirs" might be called a
kind of "gravitation" as Supervielle entitled a collection of
his own works. The stags remind us of his horses; the

time-span is of a likewise heady nature ("C'était ce qu'un autre cheval / Vingt mille siècles avant lui . . . ," as Supervielle writes on one occasion).[9] These resemblances help place the poem in the tradition of the philosophical fable; however, they leave unsaid the density of Char's thought, its non-discursive nature and, in particular, the involvement he enunciates. We have noted the even-paced measure that leads from the auditory, visual, and tactile to the conceptual, from description to self-discovery. There is none of Supervielle's cosmic distance: Char must exclaim and question, his feelings and reason whole. We find a rich number of time layers that range from the initial imperfect tense to perfect and present, before a final hypothesis that looks to future hope. But perhaps the most unusual aspect of "Les Cerfs noirs" is the envelope structure apparent from our reading: the stags are framed by the hunter, hunter and stags by primitive genius, all things by the poet. His glance seizes upon the world, not to enjoy it for himself, but to uncover yet again, like Orion, its infinite resources and those of the human imagination. The lines provide a superb illustration of Char's architectural skill, in necessary relationship to the widening circles that implicate him in the object—painting or nature—which becomes his splendidly revealing likeness.

If Breuil found several happy formulations to describe Lascaux, the title he gave the first major figure on the left

---

[9] "It was what another horse / Twenty thousand centuries before it . . ." (Jules Supervielle: "Dans la forêt sans heures," *Le Forçat innocent*, Paris, Gallimard, 1930). Supervielle is the only living poet Char mentions in his earliest collection. To him he dedicates "Progressivement sur la passe" (*Les Cloches sur le cœur*, p. 45) in which the affinity of tone and imagery is clear:

Est-ce retour à la vie quand la minute
Noyée bat comme un cœur
Au cœur d'un marbre

("Is it a return to life when the minute, / Drowned, beats like a heart / In the heart of a block of marble").

side of the main chamber is among the less fortunate. He called it "The Unicorn," emphasizing the legendary character of the animal that introduces a grotesque note into the frieze. But the image bears little resemblance to traditional treatments. Approximately eight feet in length, it is sharply individual in nature and mode. Char was doubtless right to declare it unnamable for, as it has been noted, it would seem to combine the bulk of a rhinoceros with the head of a Tibetan antelope. A heavy black line designates a massive body with thick legs, short tail, humped shoulders; the belly hangs low and almost touches the ground, its angular shape signifying pregnancy; the head and neck, disproportionately small, are likewise angular. Two horns instead of the usual one protrude in straight lines from the head; both are of inordinate length, the upper slightly more so than the lower, and commensurate with the length of the belly. The legs, thighs, and snout are colored, but not the body, which bears large oval spots outlined in black. All in all, the painting is teasingly enigmatic, and many explanations have been given, even to the point of considering the beast as a man disguised for the celebration of some cult. However, Bataille underlines what he takes to be "utter inscrutability" and "utter foreignness," which for him—and for Char—is the keynote of this image as of the sacred.[10]

LA BÊTE INNOMMABLE

La Bête innommable ferme la marche du gracieux
    troupeau, comme un cyclope bouffe.
Huit quolibets font sa parure, divisent sa folie.
La Bête rote dévotement dans l'air rustique.
Ses flancs, bourrés et tombants sont douloureux, vont
    se vider de leur grossesse.
De son sabot à ses vaines défenses, elle est
    enveloppée de fétidité.

[10] *Lascaux*, p. 62.

Ainsi m'apparaît dans la frise de Lascaux, mère
    fantastiquement déguisée,
La Sagesse aux yeux pleins de larmes.[11]

The poem follows an allegorical mode. On the other side
of bathos, alienation, suffering, tears, Char leads us, like
Valéry's Pythia, to Wisdom—"Voici parler une Sagesse.
. . ." A path is cleared by way of a new and disconcerting
language. In the case of Valéry the octosyllabic *dizain* is imbued with energy, charged with vociferation, bent to a
dramatic end; but the line is unbroken that moves from

---

[11] "*The Unnamable Beast*: The unnamable Beast brings up the rear of the
graceful herd like a buffoon cyclops. / Eight quibbles constitute her cloak,
divide her madness. / The Beast burps piously in the rustic air. / Her
crammed and sagging sides are sore, will be rid of their gestation. / From
her sabot to her futile tusks she is wrapped in fetidity. // Thus appears to
me in the Lascaux frieze—our mother fantastically disguised— / Wisdom
with her eyes full of tears" (*La Paroi et la Prairie*, p. 13). The original manuscript in the Fonds Doucet bears the title "La Bête innomable (sic)" and
reads:

    La bête innomable (sic) ferme la marche
        du (gracieux) troupeau gracieux comme
        un cyclope bouffe
    Elle rote dévotement dans (le plein air) (le vent)
        (le matin) l'air rustique
    Ses flancs bourrés et tombants sont douloureux,
        vont se vider (sur la mousse glacée)
        (dans la neige calleuse)
    De la corne au sabot elle est enveloppée de fétidité,
    Huit quolibets sont sa parure (la moins dérisoire)
    Ainsi m'apparaît-elle, dans la frise de Lascaux, mère
        fantastiquement déguisée
    (Souveraine et calleuse) (Il y a belle lune à parier
        qu'elle figure la plus poignante Sagesse
        et) la ride amère
    La Sagesse, la (très dramatique Sagesse)
        (plus belle figure des Sagesses)
        (aux yeux pleins de larmes gonflées en)
        (source de risée et de . . .)
        aux yeux pleins de larmes.
The structure of the poem is achieved, although lines will still be dis-
placed and the language tightened. The second last line contains a re-
gionalism ("Il y a belle lune à parier . . .") the loss of which we may regret;
but Char opted for incisive brevity.

baroque obsecration to classical transparency. Char's poem
follows quite another tack: it thrives on discontinuity, proceeds by linguistic substantiation rather than predication.
In a paratactic sequence Wisdom emerges, monstrous, re-
viled of men, its female form yet bearing witness; indeed,
its evidence is properly inescapable inasmuch as it lives
and has its being as near, and as unnamable, as the sensibility.

So it is that the beast closes the line. We know that, held
in contempt, relegated to the rear, the fate of Wisdom is to
enjoy no esteem: it neither attracts nor compels. Yet, discreetly present, coming after and not before, it is the end of
our experience, a faithfully following shadow. The initial
simile brings a mock-heroic note, an ungainly union of
Homeric adventure and Italian farce: the beast, like the fa-
bled form, is fierce and cumbersome but also clownesque.
Is not Wisdom "one-eyed," which a little deviousness can
circumvent? Looking at it, we see a burlesque gait, anach-
ronisms, awkwardnesses. Who can take it seriously?

The attitude of comic detachment is continued in line 2,
which, after the legendary trait, intermingles the abstract
and the concrete. Ostensibly it is descriptive of the spots or
spirals like so many ritual emblems; but these are concep-
tualized as verbal spluttering, circuitous argument. As
droll as a Molière notary, Wisdom has words alone to deck
it out. They appear to bring some semblance of method to
its madness like a parting in a shock of hair, yet the logic,
such as it is, fumbles woefully. Indeed, we hold Wisdom to
be tantamount to folly, until its true sense is learnt, its
ways understood.

Of almost identical length to the previous line a parallelism now recalls the opening, but the cadence goes
astray. Instead, the unlyrical nature of the description asserts itself as "Bête" is followed by "rote" and "dévotement": assonance, and the humorous juxtaposition of contrary meanings, designate Wisdom's strangeness amongst
us. Its burping in the pastoral calm—here the emphasis of

"air rustique" is purposely brusque—is far from the po-
liteness we expect of the classical Minerva: the beast puts
not only its foot wrong, but its table manners. It indulges
in digestive relief with the undivided attention that—we
tell ourselves—should be kept for better things. Yet Wisdom too can have enough, and dismiss stupidity with a
full-bodied response.

The rhythm expands once more into ungainliness; assonance and alliteration are heavy, the coordination is
cumulative in the image of the theme. For this pregnancy
does not signify joy but pain: the first clause conveys an
excessive burden, the second a straining after resolution.
The words are earthy and anatomically precise as Wisdom
bears the weight of its fertility, striving to end a travail that
can never be assuaged once and for all. The tension remains; the ripening does not end.

If the rhythm of line 5 is as broad as before, a balance is
almost reached between its two halves. Want of elegance,
however, continues to be evident in the language: in
"sabot" we find the metaphor of an unsophisticated object
so much the more homely for being single (Char is doubtless interpreting the right foreleg, which has been described as misdrawn; it is certainly straight and unrealis-
tic); the tusks are for show, not for use. The beast is essen-
tially vulnerable; it is also separate from the animals that
precede it, and from all other things, since it is in bad
odour. Yet "fétidité" indicates a Latinate emphasis that
partakes not at all of the comic or pathetic: it denotes an
extreme point of abandonment, the total inadaptation of
Wisdom to other things. Thereby the beast takes on the
ritual role of the scapegoat forced to wander and bear the
sins of a people: the height of reprobation, it still performs
a sacred and necessary function. Subtly, by the rhetorical
means of an all-inclusive construction ("de . . . à . . . ") and
the circular involvement implied in "enveloppée," the portrait is brought to a close.

Ainsi m'apparaît dans la frise de Lascaux, mère
   fantastiquement déguisée,
La Sagesse aux yeux pleins de larmes.

The last two lines provide the key by way of a personal
statement after the previous impersonal mode of address.
They build to a climax by the only line of the poem that is
not end-stopped, throwing forward the weight of the sentence by an inversion, an intervening adverbial phrase, an
apposition; they also contain the phonetic suspense
of "ainsi," "frise," "fantastiquement," "déguisée," which
prepares the final escape from insistence. Thus, without
flourish, the allegory is revealed: Wisdom, by its very nature, goes unrecognized and unsung; insulted, ill-at-ease,
it accumulates contradictions, sows comicality; it is
poignant, vulnerable, isolated. But we come to realize that,
though masked, it is the source to which we must return,
the mother weeping in sorrow, the Pietà that is the sum of
experience and future knowledge. The poem leads us to
the simplicity of this last octosyllable with the vast evoca-
tiveness of a language that calls on Judeo-Christian associations even if the tenor is wholly different. By indirections,
and in a way least expected, Char proposes a universal
and—in the final instance—deeply pathetic image.

"La Bête innommable" does not meet our expectations
of lyricism, for it makes no concessions to music and spells
out a rule of asperity. The first section is composed of lines
of twenty-one, fourteen, thirteen, nineteen and twenty-
one syllables, each end-stopped. This is followed by a coda
containing a line longer than any before it (twenty-two
syllables), not end-stopped, which leads forward to the octosyllable. Before any precise meaning there is this
strained fullness that wells up but is held immobile at each
attempt, with the exception of the last two lines, which
achieve a definitive statement. A pause occurs after line 5,
marking the transition from description to interpretation,

but other patterns lend further weight and necessity to a prosody that is seemingly fortuitous. Line 3, for example, tentatively echoes the beginning of line 1, but the parallelism is not realized; it establishes a point of suspense with respect to the more complex rhythms before and after; it also may be said to announce the brevity of the last line, and to provide implicitly a second division of the poem that counterpoints the other, this time by a division into a group of three lines followed by four. We may likewise note the series of balances that are introduced by the caesural breaks: the octosyllable of line 7 is foreshadowed in lines 2 ("Huit quolibets font sa parure. . . .") and 4 (" . . . vont se vider de leur paresse"); lines 1 and 2 contain hexasyllabic phrasings; lines 4 and 5 hendecasyllabic, lines 5 and 6 decasyllabic. A network of such metrical propositions and responses is woven, which qualifies the apparent freedom of the structure.

In conformity with the broad canvas, we find no intensive system of alliteration or assonance. Nonetheless the poem is obedient to the insistent interplay of voiced and unvoiced labials that provide a lively focus of phonetic energy. Here also there is tonal variety encompassing apparent farce (line 1), bitterness (line 3), gravity (line 4), harmonious poise (line 7). The handling of sound is throughout strongly mimetic, modeling the diverse aspects of the beast. Above all, like the metrical pattern itself, it creates a striking contrast between the complex first section and the firm coda.

Clearly, Char has forged an unorthodox vehicle for a poem whose theme is incongruency. The language mixes levels of discourse, conjoins the legendary and the vulgar, the perceptual and the conceptual. Its range may be resumed in the distance between "folie" and "Sagesse," here identified in one single figure; between "cyclope bouffe" and "mère"; between "air rustique" and "fétidité." As the adverb of the second last line indicates, we enter here the expressive domain of the fantastic, or more properly—to use a term I have advanced—that of the grotesque.

Not by abstraction, then, but by sensibility do we discover the womb and fruit of experience. The structure of the allegory shows this in the overt development of description and interpretation, body and coda, like that of a medieval portrait, but also in the subtle gradation of responses from the mock-heroic to the pathetic. Through linguistic, rhythmic, and phonetic variations, the probing eye enumerates its criticisms according to the criteria of grace, reason, manners, which show the beast sadly wanting; it also details a painful gestation and scandalous banishment. Yet beauty, intellect, breeding, decency are deceptive: having eyes we see not; and we learn that gracelessness, suffering, fetidity involve us deeply in the way of Job. The final lines are not contradictory but the end-link in a chain whereby we recognize the hidden presence and consecrated image—grotesque only with respect to conventional figurations of the sacred—of humanity's time past and still to be. Here again the Orion myth, as Char interprets it, is implicit: the desirable guide, the mythical teacher, the accumulated sum of thought and experience, is ill-perceived, unrecognized, waiting from eternity for the poet to name him, for men to understand that it is by the imagination that we live and breathe: "Orion charpentier de l'acier? Oui, lui toujours. La masse d'aventure humaine passe sous nos ponts géants."[12]

Many horses are figured on the walls of Lascaux. Several of them, with over-short legs and stocky bodies, have been likened to those of ancient Chinese paintings, and Char no doubt considered these at length. On the other hand,

---

[12] "Orion carpenter of steel? Yes, ever he. The mass of man's adventure passes underneath our bridges" ("Orion iroquois," *Aromates chasseurs*, p. 37).

Breuil was attracted to a striking polychrome horse on the left wall of the main chamber which he reproduced in his book and described as being "with black vaporous mane."[13] It seems more than feasible that this particular image—and, incidentally, Breuil's epithet—stands at the origin of "Jeune Cheval à la crinière vaporeuse," informing the happiest of the Lascaux poems.

JEUNE CHEVAL À LA CRINIÈRE VAPOREUSE

Que tu es beau, printemps, cheval,
Criblant le ciel de ta crinière,
Couvrant d'écume les roseaux!
Tout l'amour tient dans ton poitrail:
De la Dame blanche d'Afrique
A la Madeleine au miroir,
L'idole qui combat, la grâce qui médite.[14]

---

[13] Henri Breuil: *Quatre Cents Siècles d'art pariétal*, Centre d'études et de documentation préhistoriques, Montignac-Dordogne, 1952.

[14] *"Young Horse with Vaporous Mane*: How handsome you are, Spring, horse, / Filling the sky with your mane, / Covering the reeds with froth! / Your breast enfolds love entire: / From Africa's White Lady / To the mirrored Magdalene, / Combatant idol, meditative grace" (*La Paroi et la Prairie*, p. 14). The Doucet manuscript contains numerous variants:

Que tu es beau, printemps, cheval,
(Fouettant) Criblant le ciel de ta crinière!
Tout l'amour tient dans ton poitrail;
(Parmi) (Coursière) (Depuis) (De) la Dame blanche d'Afrique,
(Cours vers) (Te siffle doucement) (va tu galoperas longtemps)
(T'appelle), (et sa voix fait mal) (et de si loin)
    (et tu t'arrêtes et l'entends.)
    (Va et enlacez-vous longtemps.)
(La voix)
(Jusqu'à)
De la Dame blanche d'Afrique
(A l'Arlésienne de Van Gogh)
A la Madeleine au miroir
L'idole qui combat, la grâce qui médite

This first version is revealing in its search for an appropriate language. It hesitates on the verge of a development that would have shown the love of White Lady and horse (" . . . et enlacez-vous longtemps") but prefers the simplicity of the definitive version. We note the allusion to Van Gogh's "L'Arlésienne"; the final choice is far happier.

Here, from the beginning, lyricism prevails as the initial sequence of six octosyllables develops an isometric order that is light, urgent, responsive to the heart. We compare it with "L'Alouette," the ninth poem of the series, which inscribes a like impulse for song in similarly short compass; but instead of a complex internal structure we are given a bipartite division, with a break after line 3 that marks the end of the first sentence. Yet Char, not content to end his poem, as he might have done, on the simple symmetry of a second series of three lines, adds to the sixth line an alexandrine with a strong caesura. Thus the coda reflects in its regular hemistichs the binary shaping of the rest, emphasizing a balance that is predictable, though—as the last line demonstrates—not uniform in its every respect.

The words express an overriding sense of bounty. The vocabulary is heavily substantival and predominantly concrete: with a warm voice Char finds the language of his enthusiasm, which takes in both pagan and Christian allusions. Corresponding to this is a sound pattern that translates the exclamation of the first section by repeated plosives and dentals and the occurrence of nasal a ("printemps," "criblant," "couvrant"); the second half is characterized by the interplay of closed and open a, the frequency of i, and the intrusion of m, which, in these last lines, becomes associated with the apprehension of a secret symbolism.

But there is no time for delay: from the start the poet expresses in the most direct terms his active devotion to beauty. Passionately he cries out his commitment to a painting that is no painting but nature reborn, or born here for the first time. Although the intimate "tu" makes us expect a single subject, the words are addressed to both "printemps" and "cheval," as if each were synonymous with the other. At this point, the exclamation might end, but the participial constructions of lines 2 and 3 add to the initial attitude by depicting richness, espousing movement. All nature is suggested in the force that fills the sky with the showering abundance of a fine sieve as a night is filled with stars. Alliteration dramatizes this thought which carries over into line 3 where "couvrant" corresponds to "criblant," "écume" to "crinière." From the vastness of sky we pass to reeds covered with the froth of a colt. The scene is resplendent with light, alert with the conjunction of smallness and greatness, height and depth.

The second period follows a pattern similar to that of the first as an opening thought—to which the poet's expression might again well be limited—is stated nakedly, then amplified by way of metaphors. However, the level of discourse changes: Char interprets rather than describes and discovers what was implicit in the previous words. The horse, the season, is the emblem of love. A microcosm resumes not only animal joy and natural exuberance but, by the transition that line 4 skillfully accomplishes, human tenderness as well. The visual image still prevails as the use of "ton poitrail" shows, but now it is linked to the symbolic imagination.

For Char, the Lascaux painting was first of all as present as nature itself. Yet he was led back from nature to art. Calling on his keenest sense of a love profound and enduring, he turns to the range of art works that go from primitive man to Georges de la Tour—from an Africa seemingly beyond history to the sober calm and spiritual aura of seventeenth-century France. We know that the White Lady, a sister to Lascaux, is one of the several rock paintings to be found in the Tsisab Ravine of the Brandberg massif in southwest Africa. First discovered in 1917, the gallery was meticulously described and copied by Breuil. The group is done in several styles but is dominated by the figure of a striding huntress with white beads in her red hair. The top of her body and her arms are red and decorated with darker markings, and her lower torso and legs are white. She carries in her right hand a long bow and iron-tipped arrows, in her left a white cup-like object on a

stalk. Breuil surmised that she was perhaps a visitor from
the far-off Mediterranean. Or was she not, as Char divines,
a dynamic protectress and legendary savior, an ideal image
of elegance and action, of purposefulness and charm—a
female Orion? As for the "Madeleine au miroir," we need
nothing by way of explanation after our reading of
"Madeleine à la veilleuse." No doubt the most famous of
La Tour's four depictions of the Magdalene (also called the
Fabius "Magdalene"), now in Washington, it represents
the saint hesitating between her past and the contempla-
tive life. Char has spoken elsewhere of the particular virtue
the painting has for him; and alongside him today at
L'Isle-sur-Sorgue, as before in the maquis, he has reproductions of La Tour's Magdalenes, their silence rich with
suggestion.

Thus "Jeune Cheval à la crinière vaporeuse" brings together nature and eternal art, description and symbolism.
It calls with equal ardor on the primitive and the refined; it
links the male and the female—spring and horse, White
Lady and Magdalene—in one encompassing idea. A final
formulation of this encounter of contraries is proposed in
the last line which refers back to the dynamism of the
White Lady and the motionlessness of the Magdalene in
order to link them: breaking with the previous meter, its
caesura exactly balanced, an alexandrine offers the union,
evocatively determined in the previous lines, of object and
idea, aggressiveness and grace.

Char's love-song moves us by the total commitment of a
sensibility which, by means of a Lascaux painting, discovers nature's freshness, then the universal presence of
art, and finally a complex dualism. Spring's beauty, the
bounding energy of a colt, bears the name of love; but love
is also the name the poet gives no less fervently to the images of his artistic admiration. There is no conflict between
the two despite the breadth of reference to sky and reeds,
energy and calm, combat and meditation, figure and na-

ture. On the contrary, the one requires the other, each nourishing the sense whereby man seeks to live: art is not sufficient unto itself but fires our response to nature, and nature quickens art. Such a pattern of complementarity is written into the substance of "Jeune Cheval à la crinière vaporeuse," which reaches its climax in words neither concrete nor allegorical but symbolic, that possess, after the fashion of our most enduring symbols, the ambiguity of the sacred, the salvational power of thought magically virginal.

By a last poem the Lascaux series achieves heightened perspective and resonance. Char reminds us that the four previous images, and his reflections on them, are not ornamental but privileged signs, the incised evidence of a continuing struggle with fate, inhumanity, disorder. Today, no less then before, is a time of cruelty, yet the poet tells of rebirth. Each of the Lascaux paintings, far from illustrating an idealized past—"Cette espérance de retour est la pire perversion de la culture occidentale, sa plus folle aberration"[15]—is as present as soul and body, its drama ever enacted. "Transir" speaks with a moral commitment that subsumes bison, stags, unnamable beast, colt: an ice-age is again upon us, our days are somber, but austerity is our chance. From despair comes this iconography of hope, from mortal chill warmth. As Char writes in one of his most recent collections: "S'il te faut repartir, prends appui contre une maison sèche;" again: "Porteront rameaux ceux dont l'endurance sait user la nuit noueuse qui précède et suit l'éclair."[16]

This, then, is the lesson he draws from Lascaux, which

[15] "That hope for a return is the worst perversion of Western culture, its maddest delusion" (*Recherche de la base et du sommet*, p. 131).

[16] "If you must set out again, brace yourself on a dry house" ("Contre une maison sèche," *Le Nu perdu*); "They shall carry branches, whose endurance can wear out the knotted night that precedes and follows the lightning-flash" ("Le Nu perdu", *ibid.*, p. 31).

he formulates in dynamic terms. He turns to poetic prose in the same way as for the concluding poem of the sequence given over to the prairie, yet no styles are less alike. Instead of a single paragraph offering an elegiac narrative, "Transir" is divided into six short paragraphs at furthest remove from discursiveness; instead of an intimate scheme of recollection, we find these notes, an elliptic last will and testament that has no space or time for anything but its own ardent conviction.

TRANSIR

Cette part jamais fixée, en nous sommeillante, d'où jaillira DEMAIN LE MULTIPLE.

L'âge du renne, c'est-à-dire l'âge du souffle. O vitre, ô givre, nature conquise, dedans fleurie, dehors détruite!

Insouciants, nous exaltons et contrecarrons justement la nature et les hommes. Cependant, terreur, au-dessus de notre tête, le soleil entre dans le signe de ses ennemis.

La lutte contre la cruauté profane, hélas, vœu de fourmi ailée. Sera-t-elle notre novation?

Au soleil d'hiver quelques fagots noués et ma flamme au mur.

Terre où je m'endors, espace où je m'éveille, qui viendra quand vous ne serez plus là? (*que deviendrai-je* m'est d'une chaleur presque infinie).[17]

[17] "*Mortal Chill*: That part never fixed, slumbering within us, from which will spring forth TOMORROW THE MANIFOLD. / The age of reindeer, that is, the age of breath. O window-pane, O hoar-frost, nature conquered, flowering within, destroyed without. / Carefree, we rightly exalt, and exactly oppose, nature and men. Nevertheless, terror, above our heads, the sun is entering the sign of its enemies. / The struggle with profane cruelty, alas, a winged ant's desire. Will it be our novation? / In the winter sunshine a few tied bundles of sticks, and on the wall my flame. / Earth where I go to sleep, space where I wake, who will come when you are there no more? (*what shall I become* is for me of almost infi-

In its infinitive form the title conveys the unaccom-
plished state that is signified: we ourselves now occupy an
instant of transition that, whether we realize it or not, is
akin to death. We are "passing over," numbed by a glacial
malevolence. Yet there is in each man a febrility, a vital
diversity we variously call imagination, sensibility, love. It
is his invincible part, not subject to external tyrannies, and,
as Char announces with confidence in the first lines of his

---

nite warmth)" (*La Paroi et la Prairie*, pp. 17-18). The Doucet manuscript
shows the following variants:

> Cette part jamais (forcée) fixée, en nous
> sommeillante, d'où jaillira *demain le*
> *multiple*.
> L'âge de renne, c'est-à-dire l'âge du souffle.
> O vitre, ô givre, nature conquise, dedans
> fleurie, dehors détruite!
> Insouciants, nous exaltons et contrecarrons
> justement la nature et les hommes.
> Cependant, terreur, au-dessus de
> notre tête, la lune devient solaire,
> le soleil entre dans le signe
> de ses ennemis. (Continuons.)
> La lutte contre la cruauté profane
> (a cessé d'être) n'est plus un vœu
> de fourmi ailée. Elle est
> (devenue) notre (obligation)
> novation.
> Au soleil d'hiver quelques fagots
> noués et (notre) (mon) (amour),
> ma flamme du mur.
> Terre où je m'endors, espace où
> je m'éveille, que deviendrai-je
> (qui viendra) quand vous ne
> serez plus là. Gué, aux jambes
> cassées, je sais et je le dis, quelle
> est ma direction.
> (*Que deviendrai-je*, m'est chaleur
> et presque infini).

It is clear that little remains to be corrected. Char will prefer "fixée" to
"forcée," vitality to virginity; he will eliminate the hallucinatory "la lune
devient solaire"; he will tighten the fourth paragraph. Most significant of
all, the sentence "Gué, aux jambes cassées . . ." is erased without trace,
since the river to be forded, the direction to be taken, are already elliptically known.

poem, it will find expression. From our present the future
will be born like fire from ice, water from rock, spring from
winter, waking from sleep.

The subject of the subordinate clause ("DEMAIN LE
MULTIPLE"), pointed up by inversion, is a concept that
takes on material force by way of capitalization. This is the
vision of a new time that, in the image of man's inner vitality, is multiple since it corresponds to his every dream for
the future. Although its formulation echoes certain hermetic texts, it designates a world remade to match the
abundance of poetry within the self. To be single is to be
definable, therefore dead or dying; whereas poetry, man's
hope and love, is plurivalent and ever reconstituted.

An abrupt change in time scale comes after the predic-
tion, metaphorical allusion after abstraction. The age of
reindeer is evoked without explanation, and the definition
that follows is equally elliptic. But this conjunction of terms
proposes a time that is both prehistorical and as close as
the body itself. "Souffle" signifies our reduction to the essential: we become aware of the rhythm we originate without realizing it; it is the meter of aspiration and respiration,
the life-breath of renewal to which we consciously turn in a
period as hostile as another ice-age.

Following this ellipsis, an invocation translates in still
more nervous rhythms and with insistent sonority
("vitre," "givre," "conquise," "fleurie," "détruite") the
contradictions of a present in which man is forced back on
his own resources. We find the tension between exterior
and interior as window-pane and hoar-frost offer twin aspects of the same reality. Nature is overcome by cold but,
in the austerity of a retreat, the destruction outside is seen
in the form of flowers, a pattern on the pane, a marvelous
blossom.

In the third paragraph there are for the first time main
verbs in the two sentences. The poet relaxes his tone
momentarily in order to express a carefree time and our

way of living with it. We consider our relation to nature
and men, describe it in its various aspects. As brothers or
as adversaries, we praise and oppose, and discover ourselves with respect to a world that appears sure. But such a
time is not for now since the terms of relationship have al-
tered. Instead of our previous freedom of maneuver a fatal
transition has occurred, so that the age is out of joint. With
the ineluctability of the wheeling stars, or a climatic
change, terror is written in our destiny. "Cependant" answers "insouciants"; an agitated composition in four parts
succeeds the more relaxed two-part sentence; the impersonal force of the sun replaces the personal "nous." This
reversal of forces is also conveyed by the reflection of
"justement" in "au-dessus de notre tête": the adverb signifies a classical justice; yet, in the second half of the line, it
is no longer man who metes out judgment but—as force-
fully as midday—a moment of stellar crisis to which man is
tributary.

The fourth paragraph turns again to an elliptic style, and
to the tense struggle with an age of chaos. A tragic epoch
will be not suffered but met head-on in an attempt, fraught
with danger, to assert the humane. On one side is man's
desire, the agitation of a winged ant; on the other, inhumanity, for which nothing is sacred. In opposition, then,
lies our hope. For the poet fragility is strength, and his
voice rises in a question that is an implicit declaration of
faith. He looks to this future, speculates, proposes another
world to be; but the word used to evoke the vision ("novation") implies a contractual obligation wholly pertinent in
the case of moral rebirth, an elaboration of present and future obligations to nature and men.

Allusively, the penultimate paragraph depicts an austere
present. Instead of the many abstract terms of the previous
lines Char names a personal poverty (for the first time, the
first person singular is used) that corresponds to the poverty of nature: the sun is that of the winter of the soul, and

man's only companions are a meager fuel and fire. (No doubt we are right to recall the words of one of Eluard's most memorable poems, which speak from a situation of similar nakedness: "Je fis un feu, l'azur m'ayant abandonné / Un feu pour être son ami. . . . ")[18] This is in accord with the elemental; against the overwhelming expanse of cold, man lights the flame that is his strength, his tenderness. The line is urgent, yet moves without punctuation in a single unemphatic span of fifteen syllables, its stylistic means no less restrained than the sobriety it evokes.

Nevertheless brevity yields in the last paragraph to the lyrical invocation of earth and space. Rhythmic alternation is conveyed as the poet declares his attachment to the vehicle that transports him, the milieu in which he has his being. The optimism that commands his poem is found again as "je m'endors" (we recall "sommeillante" in the first line) is followed by "je m'éveille" (we remember the complementary "jaillira"). Things will disappear but there is no end, for a new heaven and earth will be seen. With no less fervor than a Christian, Char envisages a consummation that does not close but begins anew. To this death and rebirth of the world there corresponds the balance of the self's death and rebirth, for death too is a becoming. The periphrasis *"que deviendrai-je"* expresses a mortality from which all terror has been exhausted; it signifies not only acceptance, but reconciliation. The future is sure, warmth vanquishes the weight of destiny. Yet if hope is the stronger, it cannot, and must not ("presque infinie"), extinguish our awareness of evil, our unceasing need for will, effort, desire.

Written with an almost breathless energy, "Transir" articulates a vision whose law is ellipsis. It is based on the sudden telescoping of time-frames, emotions, thoughts,

---

[18] "I made a fire, the sky having abondoned me / A fire to be its friend. . . ." (Paul Eluard: "Pour vivre ici," *Choix de poèmes*, Paris, Gallimard, 1951, p. 19).

on the tension between present and future. Its language is allusive, but it achieves dramatic force by sentences without main verbs like so many exclamations (in five cases out of ten), verbs of movement and becoming ("jamais fixée," "jaillira," "entre," "viendra," "deviendra"), interjections, questions, short rhythmical parallelisms. All is multiple and mobile as man and his fateful familiar, nature—hoarfrost, sun, flame, wood, earth, air—wage a common struggle for renewal. And this action is not gratuitous since it implicates the reader from the start: the first four paragraphs speak in our name ("en nous," "nous exaltons et contrecarrons," "notre tête," "notre novation"); the last two provocatively offer, in the face of death and destruction, the immolation of the self. Yet, as we noticed in our reading, there is an internal order in each paragraph that spells out the antagonisms of inwardness and outwardness, time and space. The binary vision goes from confidence in the future to present realism; from awareness of change to tentative hope; from resolution to a final affective acceptance by way of fire and warmth.

Thus "Transir" is vastly different from "La Minutieuse," which serves as its equipoise at the end of *La Paroi et la Prairie*. On the other hand, both have direct antecedents in Rimbaud's *Illuminations*; in particular, with respect to "Transir," one thinks of poems such as "Dévotion" which show similar use of dramatic ellipsis. The reader may, however, be conscious of other accents distant in time, of a properly mystical nature, that have been wrenched from the night of anguish and exultation. "Transir" possesses a Pascalian radiance, its intensity a passionate credo addressed not to Christ but to man—"toujours à naître," as Char expresses it in the first of the Lascaux poems.

In an epigram brilliantly grasped in sensible terms Char now finds a transcendent passion for which nothing is more imperative than the gift of self. Into the external world he

reads the image of sacrifice, which becomes the first poem
of the series spoken under a Mediterranean sky. And these
words carry with them the full weight of Char's œuvre, so
much of which might provide a commentary on "Le
Taureau." We think for example of certain passages that
delineate facets of the same emotional fancy: "Terre
mouvante, horrible, exquise et condition humaine
hétérogène se saisissent et se qualifient mutuellement," he
writes in *Partage formel.* "La poésie se tire de la somme exal-
tée de leur moire";[19] in *Rougeur des matinaux*: "Enfin si tu
détruis, que ce soit avec des outils nuptiaux";[20] in *Commune Présence*: "Certains êtres ont une signification qui
nous manque. Qui sont-ils? Leur secret tient au plus pro-
fond du secret même de la vie. Ils s'en approchent. Elle les
tue. Mais l'avenir qu'ils ont ainsi éveillé d'un murmure, les
devinant, les crée. O dédale de l'extrême amour!"[21] Above
all, of course, it recalls for us "Homme-Oiseau mort et
Bison mourant." However "Le Taureau" takes on particular relief because of the economy of its language, its
rhythmical and phonetic power, and, most especially, the
singular conjunction it proposes in form and theme of an
unfathomable image of desire with the conscious will.

LE TAUREAU

Il ne fait jamais nuit quand tu meurs,
Cerné de ténèbres qui crient,
Soleil aux deux pointes semblables.

[19] "Earth, moving, horrible, exquisite and heterogeneous human condition clasp each other and are mutually qualified. Poetry is drawn from
the exalted sum of their moire" ("Partage formel," *Poèmes et Prose choisis*,
p. 222).
[20] "Finally, if you destroy, let it be with instruments nuptial" ("Rougeur des matinaux," *ibid.*, p. 242).
[21] "Certain beings have a significance we lack. Who are they? Their secret depends on the deepest point of life's own secret. They draw near to
it. It kills them. But the future they have thus awakened with a murmur
divines and creates them. O maze of extreme love!" (*ibid.*, p. 191).

Fauve d'amour, vérité dans l'épée,
Couple qui se poignarde unique parmi tous.[22]

Like three other poems of *La Paroi et la Prairie*, "Le Taureau" is composed in free verse. It contains two octosyllables and lines of nine, ten, and twelve syllables. Yet this apparent irregularity is countervailed by a hexasyllabic measure which imposes its balance (6/3, 6/2, 2/6, 4/6, 6/6). Without a uniform meter, it thus offers a rhythm recurring and ultimately dominant.

The texture of sound is especially close. At the opposite pole from mellifluent alliteration, it establishes an interplay of plosives and dentals that conveys high emotional intensity. This is reinforced by the vowel scheme, characterized by the frequency of i and open and closed e and, on the other hand, by the almost complete absence of nasals. A line such as the final one, exploiting as it does the pattern of consonants and vowels already found in what precedes, creates a vigorous series of correspondences across the caesural pause, thus translating the drama into a kind of phonetic equivalent.

The first line is an expression of complete faith as the use of "jamais" excludes the night and pathos that accompany death. The bull's slaying, felt as an illumination, is raised to the realm of ideas by verbal generality: the mode of address denotes both the poet's communion with the bull and the bull's eternal nature since, like a god, it ritually dies and is forever reborn. After this confident opening, the second line shows the tension from which illumination springs : in an adjectival phrase that evokes a siege and an obsession, it points to the darkness that is the counterpart of light. The rhythm has changed from the flat rapidity of the first line to a greater deliberateness, which corresponds

---

[22] "*The Bull*: It is never night when you die, / Circled by shrieking shadows, / Sun with two like points. // Beast of love, sword's truth, / Murderous duo unique before all" (*La Paroi et la Prairie*, p. 21).

to the metaphorical emphasis of "cerné" and "ténèbres." The bull is a city invested by the enemy, a hero plagued by fate. "Ténèbres," in particular, introduces a tragic level, confirmed in the relative clause by harsh alliteration and assonance and an auditory image: the shades are so many harpies carrying out cruel torments.

The section closes on an apposition that develops the opening line but places it in sharp contrast to the second. The rhythm gives full accent to "soleil": taking on the resonance of the solar myths, the bull is identified with radiance, warmth, renewal. Yet this is no ordinary scene, for the transpierced sun is none such as we know but the sign of a glory attained in violence. It translates the union of bull and sword, these two deadly points that meet like predestined lovers.

The three parts of the final section, even more condensed than those of the preceding lines, resume the drama in two abstract phrases, then reformulate it in a striking apposition. The rhythm becomes gradually more assured from the first words, which evoke the animal force and presence of love: the bull sacrifices its all to a fatal encounter. The words that follow take up the time-honored image of a corrida as the moment of truth par excellence, placing the abstract term "vérité" alongside "amour" as the twin blade of this confrontation. The asymmetrical disposition of the two phrases imposes a precipitate movement, which is further accentuated by the four occurrences of closed e like a single insistent note.

At the beginning of the last line "couple" sums up the duality of "fauve" and "épée," "amour" and "vérité," and the previous "deux pointes semblables." It is an alliance realized by way of death. The alliteration of "couple" and "qui" echoes that of "qui crient" in line 2 with the same phonetic suggestion of shrillness. Yet from this slaying ("se poignarde" recalls "pointes" semantically and phonetically) emerges the unity, and uniqueness, that are ar-

ticulated in the last three words. The meeting with death
achieves a supreme instant, while its significance is an
ideal projection.

Char's words are of thanatos and eros, sunlight and
shadow. Incisive, direct, they are here developed with
such concentration that they take on exceptional weight.
Of the two dramatic statements that compose the poem,
the second has no main verb, so that it approaches the register of an exclamation: the first gradually builds to a
climax, its impact growing from an initial simplicity to the
richly dramatic metaphor of line 3. We observe however
that, although the two sentences are of different contour
and length, each is made up of three segments that constitute a complementarity within the asymmetrical form. "Le
Taureau" thus establishes a varied rhythm that possesses a
number and direction of its own; it weaves a dynamic
sound pattern dependent on internal rhyme, assonance,
and alliteration; it contains a structural balance founded on
a ternary progression of each of the two sections. But it
also calls on our experience of the bull-fight, its fury, its
color, its enactment of an age-old ritual; and this in turn
reaches to some of the most vital tensions of our sensibility. The two abstract words in line 4 reveal the allegorical
dimension, emphasize its universal import. In the same
way, the last equally abstract phrase ascribes to the drama
the value of an emotional absolute that is a peak surpas-
sing all others. The tragic encounter is the occasion for a
discovery that, like Orion's hunt, can serve as our guide
and exemplar.

The next *fascinant*, "La Truite" brings together a series of
details that point to the notion of love. It is ordered with
plastic skill similar to that of "Le Taureau," spelling out a
formal necessity that controls the single sentence. But the
poem leads beyond reason—indeed, it destroys substantial
outline—and conveys a meaning of the heart. Tenderness
is the interanimating force; it engenders the magic trans-

mutation that nature can suggest to someone such as Char, who voices a change without price. "L'orage," he writes, "a deux maisons. L'une occupe une brève place sur l'horizon; l'autre, tout un homme suffit à peine à la contenir."[23] It is this other clear storm of the spirit that the poem conjures up for us.

LA TRUITE

Rives qui croulez en parure
Afin d'emplir tout le miroir,
Gravier où balbutie la barque
Que le courant presse et retrousse,
Herbe, herbe toujours étirée,
Herbe, herbe jamais en répit,
Que devient votre créature
Dans les orages transparents
Où son cœur la précipita?[24]

Here we find an unemphatic structure and sense rather than the force of "Le Taureau." A man speaks to natural objects, and his animism is devoid of excess or strain. His voice models itself on the variegated image of the trout as it weaves a way among eddies of sound and sense, diverse but not diffuse. All is uttered in the present tense until the last verb, which points to a disappearance and a secret action even now taking place. Char uses the imagery of clothing ("parure," "presse," "retrousse," "étirée"), of agitated movement ("croulez," "presse," "jamais en répit," "précipita"), of tenderness ("votre créature," "son cœur") in order to compose the emblem of rigor overcome and of

[23] "The storm has two mansions. One occupies a brief space on the horizon; the other can hardly be contained by one man" ("Avec Braque, peut-être, on s'était dit . . . ," *Commune Présence*, p. 209).
[24] "*The Trout*: River-banks that crumble to fill / The mirror with a ruffled raiment, / Gravel where the stammering boat / Is pulled and tugged by the current, / Grass, grass, that is forever combed, / Grass, grass, that is never at rest, / What is betiding your creature / Amid the transparent tempests / Into which her heart propelled her?" (*La Paroi et la Prairie*, p. 22).

love victorious. "La Truite" is, in modest terms, a beauti-
fully constructed poem, its tone poised, its manner simple.

The nine octosyllables are unrhymed, but make use of
internal echoes to build a closely knit pattern of sound. The
insistence of hard c, post-vocalic r, i, and ou introduces the
combined sharpness and harmony that mark the poem;
lines 5 and 6, by identical rhythms which serve as a kind of
refrain, stress the informing lyricism. The poem is first and
foremost a song, a melodic line moving swiftly and as a
single substance on its unbroken period and even meter,
and composed of four clearly articulated parts: three invocations of two lines each to river-banks, gravel, and grass,
and a final question that poses an unanswered riddle.

From the beginning, the visual and emotional are joined.
The river with its reflected banks speaks not only to the eye
but to the heart, for a magical transformation is taking
place on the mirrored surface: definite outline is being reduced to softness, earth and rock to adornment. It is an
image that suggests in dynamic terms ("croulez") the details of a natural scene; but the intention that is read into it
by the poet is determinedly human. Headlong pursuit is
evoked by the adverbial phrase ("Afin de . . . "), a force
thrusting one element toward another.

Again, in lines 3 and 4, the auditory images contained in
the repeated alliteration and assonance ("balbutie,"
"barque"; "que," "courant"; "presse," "retrousse"), and
the use of the verb "balbutie" itself, precisely convey the
depth of silence in a rural landscape. But this movement is
also that of another gentleness, the sinuous caress of water
on moored boat.

The third step in the anaphoric development is the most
musical as the poet's words espouse their object. The four
occurrences of "herbe" enunciate in sound and sight a
humble image drawn to an invisible goal. In the same way,
"toujours étirée" and "jamais en répit" are rhythmically

balanced, although "toujours" and "jamais" suggest by their polarity the nervous energy that commands the scene. An imperious wind holds sway, transforming grass into the blades of erotic desire.

Now, ending these invocations, the poem puts a question that receives no response but implies an answer. The act of becoming is the mystery of love in which the "cœur" of line 9 plays the essential part. The heart has wrought this sudden and reckless surrender, succinctly expressed by the past definite tense ("précipita"); the trout has been united with the element that nourishes and enshrines it. Resuming the entire gentleness of the poem, the oxymoron of the penultimate line proposes an alliance of passion and clarity that is the hidden key. In addition, this particular epithet has personal significance for Char, who gave the title "Les Transparents" to one of his poetic scenarios so as to designate the legendary figures of the Provençal countryside—various, immaterial, undying. The poet has, then, depicted an emblem that founds his dialectic, justifies the hunt, inspires its trajectory. "Dans nos ténèbres", he writes, "il n'y a pas une place pour la Beauté. Toute la place est pour la Beauté".[25]

"Le Serpent" is a witty poem, ample yet suave, which discovers a wisdom in its ironic structure, its modern fashioning of a courtly mode. It provides the memorable expression of a vital "marginality" at the heart of Char's work and the incentive of his ethic: "Moi qui jouis du privilège," he writes, "de sentir tout ensemble accablement et confiance, défection et courage . . . "; and again: "Nous ne pouvons vivre que dans l'entrouvert, exactement sur la ligne hermétique de partage de l'ombre et de la lumière. Mais nous sommes irrésistiblement jetés en

---

[25] "Within our shadows there is not a single place for Beauty. The whole place is for Beauty" ("Feuillets d'Hypnos," *Poèmes et Prose choisis*, p. 66).

avant. Toute notre personne prête aide et vertige à cette poussée."[26]

LE SERPENT

Prince des contresens, exerce mon amour
A tourner son Seigneur que je hais de n'avoir
Que trouble répression ou fastueux espoir.

Revanche à tes couleurs, débonnaire serpent,
Sous le couvert du bois et en toute maison.
Par le lien qui unit la lumière à la peur,
Tu fais semblant de fuir, ô serpent marginal![27]

For his meter Char here chooses an elevated vehicle. His seven alexandrines are rhymeless if we exclude the weak homophony of "n'avoir" and "espoir" in lines 2 and 3; yet the caesurae are regularly observed and indicate a decorum that already conveys in part the character of his snake. The sound pattern complements this measure by creating a sensuous atmosphere. Sibilants are dominant, as befits the subject, but we also note the poet's special delight in assonance: thus, "exerce," "débonnaire,"

[26] "I who enjoy the privilege of feeling at one and the same time dejection and confidence, desertion and courage . . ." ("Biens égaux," *Poèmes et Prose choisis*, p. 70); "We can only live in the intermediate, precisely on the dividing-line between shadow and light. But we are borne irresistibly onwards. Our whole being provides sustenance and vertigo for this thrust." ("Dans la marche," *Commune Présence*, p. 266).

[27] "*The Snake*: Prince of ways counter, ply my love / So it foils its Lord whose offering I hate / Of vexed hindrance only, or flaunty hope. // Revenge for your colors, debonair snake, / Under cover of wood and in every house. / By the bond that joins daylight and fear, / You pretend to flee, frequenter of margins!" (*La Paroi et la Prairie*, p. 23). The original version of the first stanza of "Le Serpent" as published in *Cahiers du Sud* (No. 150, 1950) and, subsequently, in the plaquette *Quatre Fascinants*, *La Minutieuse* (Paris, 1951), reads:

Prince des contresens, fasses (sic) que mon amour
En exil analogue à ton bannissement
Echappe au vieux Seigneur que je hais d'avoir pu,
Après l'avoir troublé, en clair le décevoir.

"serpent," "couvert"; "amour," "tourner," "troubler," "couvert," "toute"; "Seigneur," "couleurs," "peur"; "contresens," "revanche," "serpent," "semblant." The result is a structure with considerable depth of resonance and strength of line.

The scheme Char has adopted follows that of the envois to prince and protector found in medieval ballads. This is borne out by the tone as the poet addresses himself directly three times to the snake in the three sentences that make up his poem. At the beginning a noble invocation is used, which also carries with it a strain of mock seriousness; on the second occasion the courtly aspect is again allied to the comic ("débonnaire serpent"), the position of the adjective emphasizing the poet's sympathetic indulgence; finally, the last words combine a dignified apostrophe with an epithet that is very much tongue-in-cheek. So, at far remove from both "Le Taureau" and "La Truite," mingling eloquence and a saving smile, "Le Serpent" manages its "low" theme with a fine discrimination. Yet Char plays off the allegorical against the natural and opts for the latter in the second half of his poem: instead of the extremes of chastisement and hope, he prefers a middle road, and where the first section makes use of dramatic contrast ("amour," "je hais"; "trouble répression," "fastueux espoir"), the other does not oppose but conjoins ("sous le couvert du bois et en toute maison"; "le lien qui unit la lumière à la peur").

As in the other poems we have examined, the form is articulated with precision. We find a ternary scheme that first (lines 1 to 3) exposes the help the poet seeks from a legendary presence. His diction is sonorous as he praises the byways of the serpent, its perverse liberty that refuses to pursue the roads of the Lord. The invocation to the "Prince des contresens" is splendid for its mixture of ceremoniousness and humor, which is continued by the imperative "exerce," inhabitual in this context, whose preciosity is muted by the familiar mode of address. Likewise, the manner in which love and hate are linked is a further token of the poet's espousal of indirections in the manner of the serpent. In the third line the language echoes medieval allegory in expressing the arbitrary antagonism within man's destiny as promulgated by the Lord. Alongside the undulations of the snake, God's fiat is bombastic.

The second section (lines 4 and 5) brings a change. No longer is the poet imagining a legendary struggle of his own; instead, he abandons his personal involvement in order to turn wholly toward the snake and celebrate it. He takes up the vocabulary of chivalry and announces a triumph: the serpent has become a self-assured knight whose colors are the pennant of victory. Yet this is the contrary of the Lord's pompous exhibitionism ("fastueux"). It is discreet, *terre à terre*, finding a hidden path in wood and house, silently present in a diversity of places. The words acquire peculiar relief for being placed after the eloquence of line 4 and of the first section.

A similar kind of verbal contrast is found in the third and final section. Line 6 expresses in abstract language a universal bond in which Apollo does not confront Dionysos, nor sunshine darkness: on the contrary, Char proposes in the likeness of the serpent a symbolic ambiguity as light touches on fear, day's calm on disquietude; and this he transforms in the last line into a familiar and immediate utterance that shows his complicity with an animal in which being and seeming are at odds. The snake is not flight but semblance of flight, for perseverance and courage make its superiority. The final apostrophe "ô serpent marginal" brings together, as I have suggested, the double focus that characterizes the poem, combining distance and familiarity. After the princely vocative Char's epithet conveys the physical and moral in-between-ness that is the snake's nature, and its lesson. It represents, not a refusal to take sides, but an impassioned awareness of polarities, a lucidity that steadfastly holds to its truth while mindful of encompassing anguish, a wisdom worthy of the paradoxes of love, hope, desire.

Nothing appears to be regular about the versification of "L'Alouette," not even a recurring meter, which in "Le Taureau," despite the varying length of the verse, constitutes an important structural element. Indeed, it is the freest of the poems of this second part of *La Paroi et la Prairie*, creating an atmosphere of exuberant spaciousness with its successive lines of fourteen, seventeen, fifteen and eleven syllables. At the end of lines 1 and 3 ("jour," "route"), assonance provides a pause and a balance before the conclusion, but we find no strongly cohesive consonantal system. Here, on the contrary, alliteration is avoided in favor of the insistence of one vowel, open "e," found thirteen times. This becomes a phonetic sostenuto lending eloquent breadth to the diction and supporting the strong rhythms imposed by the caesuras.

L'ALOUETTE

Extrême braise du ciel et première ardeur du jour,
Elle reste sertie dans l'aurore et chante la terre agitée,
Carillon maître de son haleine et libre de sa route.

Fascinante, on la tue en l'émerveillant.[28]

The poem comprises two sentences as in "Le Taureau"; as in "Le Taureau" also a lapidary epigram proposes what we may term the protasis and apodosis of a thought. A ternary rhythm reigns in each part, the first comparatively relaxed, the second tense. In the first section two apposi-

---

[28] "*The Lark*: Extreme ember of the sky and first fire of day, / She stays, a jewel set in the dawn, and sings earth's turmoil, / A carillon master of its breath and free to make its way. // Bewitcher, who is killed when struck with wonder" (*ibid.*, p. 24).

tions frame line 2; in like manner the adjective and participial phrase of line 4 frame subject, verb, and object. Seemingly disordered, "L'Alouette" in reality offers a marvelous economy of means.

In the first section the language is richly metaphoric. Char introduces the visual imagery of fire, sunset, dawn, of jewel and crown, then passes to the auditory imagery of song and carillon. Only in line 3 do we find abstract concepts with the allusion to mastery ("maître de son haleine") and freedom ("libre de sa route") that are ascribed to the lark. However, the last line, isolated from the previous ones, alters the tone with a formulation that is particularly effective because of its generality (the use of "on" underlines the universal nature of the statement) and, of course, because of the way "fascinante" and "émerveillant" complement each other like object and mirror. (A mirror-image—that of the "miroir à alouettes," the lark-mirror or twirl—is implied in the sense as in the shape of the line.)

None of the words is unusual in and of itself. Nevertheless we are obliged, by the artistry of rhythm, sound, and structure, and by the metaphors, to recognize the complexity of suggestion. Thus the first line cannot be read with anything but amplitude: space and time are required to grasp the paradox of this bird that is at once last and first, ember and flame, sunset and dawn. Occurring after the seventh syllable of this fourteen-syllable line, the caesura establishes a symmetrical balance; the open vowels enhance our expectancy; and the set of opposites becomes a luminous spectrum of the imagination.

Light is also evoked in the second line by way of the condensed metaphor of the word "sertie." The lark is a jewel set in the dawn, identified with the sun as the diamond with its crown; it controls its element, hovers like a fixed point in the immensity of air. Continuing to enumerate the bird's qualities, the second hemistich patterns itself by a natural progression on the cumulative coordination of the first line; now, however, a transforming activity is evoked. The lark takes for its theme the troubles that beset man and the world, changing them into the song it finds within itself, which is the breath of desire.

L'alouette à peine éclairée
Scintille et crée le souhait qu'elle chante;
Et la terre des affamés
Rampe vers cette vivante.[29]

The "blithe spirit" shows that art is a way of living with death: "Nous n'avons qu'une ressource avec la mort: faire de l'art avant elle," as Char writes in "Les Dentelles de Montmirail."[30]

The auditory image is pursued in the third line, expressing in another guise the restless brilliance suggested by the previous words, designating a music that transcends its maker. But the epithet that follows affirms sovereignty, male independence, as if the lark were a carillon ringing itself, controlling its own measure. Likewise, the next words present the further moral quality of freedom and the notion of mobility that has been excluded until now; the capacity to discover and create the future flourishes paradoxically in the impersonal art of the bells alongside the self-discipline that has just been named. Elsewhere Char will celebrate the same instinctive liberty he associates with birds: "Eté, rivière, espaces, amants dissimulés, toute une lune d'eau, la fauvette répète: 'Libre, libre, libre, libre. . . . ' "[31]

Finally, line 4 has exceptional imaginative force by its

[29] "The lark when the sun has barely come / Sparkles and creates the wish it sings; / And the earth of hungry men / Gropes toward this living thing" ("Fête des arbres et du chasseur," *Commune Présence*, p. 179).
[30] "We have only one resource with death: to make art before it does."
[31] "Summer, river, space, hidden lovers, a whole moon of water, the warbler repeats: 'Free, free, free, free. . . .' " ("Neuf Merci," *Poèmes et Prose choisis*, p. 183).

phonetic and semantic isolation; by the image it offers of a defenseless beauty destroyed; by its syntactical construction that, as we have seen, mirrors the first word in its last. The epithet "fascinante" is a strong one, and gains additional resonance from echoing the general title of a collection of poems; but it is also bound to "émerveillement," which proposes elliptically the image of the twirl used by hunters: the lark is dazzled by the bright reflection and easily caught in the nets. Deceived by those who profit from its naivety, it is drawn to its death. Fatality is conveyed in the three central words that are placed—ironically "set" like the jewel in a crown—in the midst of witchery.

This brief poem may be interpreted on many levels. It would for example be possible to refer to Mallarmé's commemorative sonnet for Edgar Allan Poe:

Du sol et de la nue hostiles, ô grief![32]

Char, we may say, depicts the struggle between bird and men, aspiration and failure, sky and earth, life and death. He proposes the metaphor of our destiny and the emblem, despite death, of hope ever reborn: "Pour l'aurore, la disgrâce c'est le jour qui va venir; pour le crépuscule c'est la nuit qui engloutit. Il se trouva jadis des gens d'aurore. A cette heure de tombée, peut-être, nous voici. Mais pourquoi huppés comme des alouettes?"[33] Other meanings suggest themselves: thus we may think of the relationship between poetry and the world. Proudly free, the poem does not reject troubled earth but turns it into song according to a man's desire. And yet this tenuous bond can be

---

[32] "Oh strife between warring soil and cloud!" (Stéphane Mallarmé: "Tel qu'en lui-même enfin l'êternitê le change . . . ," Œuvres complètes, Paris, Gallimard, Pléiade, p. 70).

[33] "For the dawn disgrace is the coming day; for twilight, engulfing darkness. Once there were dawn people. At this hour, perhaps, of decline, here we are. But why are we crested like larks?" ("Dans la marche," Commune Présence, p. 267).

broken when we transfix the words, reduce them to a program, replace the volatile and complex by a formula. The poet warns us: "Les oiseaux libres ne souffrent pas qu'on les regarde. Demeurons obscurs, renonçons à nous, près d'eux."[34] This reading opens out onto a properly moral plane that would see the lark as our sense of dignity and love, our ability to hold an upright image that, however, as history shows us every day, can be destroyed by the murderous means we have contrived: "Criminels sont ceux qui arrêtent le temps dans l'homme pour l'hypnotiser et perforer son âme."[35] These are, I think, valid interpretations, yet so rich is the imaginative power of Char's lines that further glosses would not be hard to find: they radiate from the lark—warm, colorful, exultant in Provençal sunshine—whose flight is ended abruptly. We have the multivalent image of the object of desire, the prey of Orion's hunt, which can never be captured whole for its very being is freedom; and yet—ironically—to seek to capture it is the only virtue. "L'Alouette" is, then, an epigram of exceptional density that calls on the visual, the auditory and the abstract, inviting us to respond to a "metaphysical" sensibility (using the term as for the seventeenth-century English poets), a resolute and broadly rhythmed diction, a language of multivalent signs. It is important to emphasize, as for the other poems of the group, the superb architectural sense with which the theme is handled: inside each sentence, as in the form as a whole, a masterly grasp of space is at work. Char shatters, that is to say, elaborates the image—Breton's "unshatterable kernel of night"[36]—composing a visionary ethic so much the more expressive for being found within the natural scene.

[34] "Free birds do not allow themselves to be looked at. Let us stay obscure, self-abnegating, near them" ("Les Compagnons dans le jardin," *Poèmes et Prose choisis*, p. 286).

[35] "Criminals are they who stop time in man so as to hypnotize him and perforate his soul" (*Poèmes et Prose choisis*, p. 260).

[36] "L'infracassable noyau de nuit."

To conclude his bestiary, as well as the sequence of *La Paroi et la Prairie*, Char has written a prose-poem that sends us back to the prairie animals we have encountered: the lark is here ("une alouette . . . chantait"); so is the snake ("quelque minuscule rongeur ou serpent s'échappant à la nage"); the pools and deep waters are the trout's element; and present too is the bull, now the domesticated bullock, its horns as resonant as poetry's lyre, its gravity opening the procession. Yet the beasts do not appear as before but are caught up in a single mood that explains and retrospectively justifies their previous figurations: for the central focus is tenderness, which finds in nature a fund of wonderment, a constant companion whose intimate name is woman. We recognize the special oneness Eluard called "l'Amour la Poésie"—poetry undivided from love, love inseparable from a lyricism of scrupulous materiality.

LA MINUTIEUSE

L'inondation s'agrandissait. La campagne rase, les talus, les menus arbres désunis les uns des autres s'enfermaient dans des flaques dont quelques-unes en se joignant devenaient lac. Une alouette au ciel trop gris chantait. Des bulles çà et là brisaient la surface des eaux à moins que ce ne fût quelque minuscule rongeur ou serpent s'échappant à la nage. La route encore restait intacte. Les abords d'un village se montraient. Résolus et heureux nous avancions. Dans notre errance il faisait beau. Je marchais entre Toi et cette Autre qui était Toi aussi. Dans chacune de mes mains je tenais serré votre sein nu. Des villageois sur le pas de leur porte ou occupés à quelque besogne de planche nous saluaient avec faveur. Mes doigts leur cachaient votre merveille. En eussent-ils été choqués? L'une de vous s'arrêta pour causer et pour sourire. Nous continuâmes. J'avais désormais la nature à ma droite et devant moi la route. Un bœuf au loin, en son milieu, nous précédait. La lyre de ses cornes, il me parut, tremblait. Je t'aimais. Mais je reprochais à celle qui était demeurée en chemin, parmi les habitants des maisons, de se montrer trop familière. Certes, elle ne pouvait figurer parmi nous que ton enfance attardée. Je me rendis à l'évidence. Au village la retiendraient l'école et cette façon qu'ont les communautés aguerries de temporiser avec le danger. Même celui d'inondation. Maintenant, nous avions atteint l'orée de très vieux arbres et la solitude des souvenirs. Je voulus m'enquérir de ton nom éternel et chéri que mon âme avait oublié: "Je suis la Minutieuse." La beauté des eaux profondes nous endormit.[37]

The development follows the pattern of a personal narrative that describes the crossing of a landscape in a time of

---

[37] "*The Heedful One*: The flood was rising. The open country, the mounds, the small scattered trees were enclosing themselves in pools, some of which joined to form a lake. In the overgray sky a lark was singing. Bubbles here and there were breaking the surface of the waters, unless it was some tiny rodent or snake swimming to safety. The road was still intact. The outskirts of a village were visible. Resolute and happy, we went on. In our wandering the weather was fair. I walked between You and that Other who was also You. In both of my hands I clasped your naked breast. Villagers on their doorsteps or busy at some woodwork greeted us with favor. My fingers were hiding your marvel. Would the people have been shocked? One of you stopped to chat and smile. We went on. Henceforth nature was on my right hand and the road ahead. A bullock, far off in his domain, preceded us. The lyre of his horns, it seemed to me, was trembling. I was in love with you. But I reproached the one who had tarried on the road, among those dwelling in the houses, for being too familiar. Certainly she could only represent amongst us your lingering childhood. I bowed to the facts. In the village she would be detained at the school, and by the way seasoned communities temporize with danger. Even the danger of a flood. Now we had come to the verge of very old trees and the solitude of memories. I wished to know your beloved eternal name that my soul had forgotten: 'I am the Heedful One.' The beauty of deep waters lulled up to sleep" (*La Paroi et la Prairie*, pp. 27-28). The variants contained in the first version (*Quatre Fascinants, La Minutieuse*, Paris 1951) are: "La route intacte"; "Mes doigts cachaient votre merveille."

flood. Nothing unusual is observed so that we are, for instance, far from a Surrealist anecdote such as those Char himself was writing in the early 'thirties. It suffices that the woman is near: she is the dual presence of innocence and prudence, fancy and fidelity, who yet bears the name of an attention that observes every facet of space and time. Her care transforms ordinary things into poetic ones: they are seen to have a function, to participate in a chain of events. Whereas our experience is all too frequently dull, and most often fragmentary, love alone sees and saves. A similar thought is put pithily by Voltaire: "Le temps: tout le consume, et l'amour seul l'emploie."[38]

Nevertheless, unlike Voltaire in his aphorism, Char gives a rich canvas to his poem by choosing as his frame of reference a broad landscape and, as its activating force, the age-old image of the flood. We think of the Bible, of Rimbaud; we also remember an admirable page from Char's Surrealist period "Eaux-mères."[39] But in "La Minutieuse" the image has a lyrical fullness it did not previously possess. It needs, I think, to be looked at in relation to a series of poems contemporaneous with *La Paroi et la Prairie* that express a like tenderness that subsumes past and future. One of its most moving expressions is "Marthe," a hymn of praise in honor of the restorative power of love, in which Char has recourse to the fountain as a symbol of time constantly renewed; or, as he says of the woman: "Vous êtes le présent qui s'accumule."[40] Another example is "La Sorgue" in which the stream and Yvonne, henceforth inseparable, compose the Heraclitean splendor of the eternal now. Fountain; river; but also flood: Char evokes both peril and renewal, a fatal event written in the heavens which nonetheless fashions nature in love's likeness. "Etrange exigence," he writes in "A une sérénité crispée,"

---

[38] "All things consume time, and love alone uses it."
[39] *Le Marteau sans maître*, pp. 75-79.
[40] "You are each present moment accumulating."

"que celle d'un présent qui nous condamne à vivre entre la promesse et le passé, car il est le déluge, ce déluge avec lequel, hier, notre imagination convolait."[41]

I have mentioned Rimbaud, whose "Après le déluge" and "Aube" come to mind when we consider the theme of "La Minutieuse" and the initiation it narrates. But other traits underline the same affinity: the sense of nature, the animism, the concreteness allied with abstraction, the brilliant texture of the prose. "La Minutieuse" is firmly situated in the tradition that stems from the *Illuminations;* but unlike the Surrealist texts that form part of this same poetic line, it does not include the gratuitous: indeed, gratuitousness is totally alien to it, for we find in these lines a supervening order—intellectual as well as physical. The waters are those we associate with an implicit threat, and this feeling finds expression in the last lines of "La Minutieuse" ("le danger . . . d'inondation . . . "). But there is no obvious anxiety: the self observes and accepts the waters, recognizing their inevitability yet detailing their effects with the attention we might give to the flow of poetry itself. This is an enchanted present, an imaginary time in which the four previous poems are seen similarly to move and have their being.

The octosyllabic rhythm of the first sentence will recur in four later sentences and is the basic measure of the poem. It serves to point up the second sentence, the longest (with sentence 4) of the text, in which the swelling lyrical charm of the flood is indicated by the personifications as well as by the strong assonance comparable to a rhyme of "flaque" and "lac."

Now animal life appears in which we discern a direct

[41] "Strange requirement of a present time that sentences men to live between promise and past, for it is the flood, that flood with which, a short time ago, our imagination would take flight" ("A une sérénité crispée" [deuxième version], *Cahiers du Sud,* Numbers 373-374, September-October 1963, p. 18).

echo of the lark and the snake. However somber the sky, the bird still sings; the waters too, alive with activity, play some light-hearted game of hide-and-seek like that of the trout. The use of "minuscule" after "menus" in the second sentence helps to prepare for "minutieuse," by which is designated a finely attuned attention to things small alongside the vast; or to the poem that presupposes all poetry; or to the minutes that make an ideal time; or to the many diminutive facets that constitute the meaning of love.

A road crossing the landscape shows the work of men. It obliquely introduces the lyrical self and its companions in a series of intertwined rhythms. Although movement was sketched in the first lines it is now emphasized, and happiness—that which we find in walking, or in the weather, or in women, or in the welcoming villagers—triumphs. Despite the flood, a way is open, a village with its familiar life is at hand, the sky is clear. But there are contradictions, and in them lies the seductiveness of Char's vision: the self is both strong-willed and fanciful; it advances and at the same time wanders; above all, it is accompanied by companions who are twin aspects of a single person, images of a dual self, whose identity is not defined but whose importance is underscored. Their mystery is central to the poem. We recognize the dimension of a dreamlike state in which paratactical language is its own justification; we also know, now, that the poet's words are overheard rather then heard, for they are addressed to another—the mistress and her sister-image who are not two, yet not one alone. Even gestures are ambiguous: the poet holds the women as his ardent possession, but he also explains his action a second way, as being required so as to hide from the villagers a naked beauty that would shock them. Such precision without final elucidation is the mode of the poem and, as we know, the substance of reverie.

The first half ends on a rhythm that concludes the lyrical

pattern characteristic of these lines. The self asks an unanswered question indicative of a meticulousness already
apparent in the description, which faithfully reflects the
mistress "Minutieuse." The introduction of two past definites ("s'arrêta," "continuâmes") marks an abrupt change.
Instead of forward movement there is tension between
suspense and continuity; instead of a common progress,
separation. We also observe the repetition of "pour" denoting intentionality, all trace of which has been eschewed
until this point. These elements will recur in the lines that
follow. The location of nature and road with respect to the
self is given with the care typical of a dream vision. The
bullock seems to inhabit a space of its own ("en son
milieu") like the enchanted being of some ritual ceremony.
Yet this is but one more aspect of poetry, as the horns
changed into a lyre remind us, in the same way as flood,
landscape, animals, women offer other facets of the same
single complex. If the horns of the bull in "Le Taureau"
come to mind, tragedy is here transformed into Dionysian
vibration, a music synonymous with lyricism and love.

"Je t'aimais": a direct expression of tenderness is given
for the first time in the simplest of terms. Yet we discover
simultaneously that separation from the other feminine
presence has continued: "demeurée en chemin" again
emphasizes the contrast between stasis and progression
for which the infinitive construction ("de se montrer trop
familière") ascribes an abstract causality that culminates in
the allegorical interpretation of the woman as childhood,
guilelessness, the sensibility all too readily wounded. Of
herself she does not suffice to create poetry, yet without
her poetry is verbiage. The reproach yields to understand-
ing: the poet explains the child-woman's absence by easily
comprehensible reasons. He postulates two of these, and
in so doing intermingles the concrete and the abstract, the
material and the moral, in a surprising semantic and syntactic hypallage.

The journey is complete, the goal attained. The concrete and abstract are again affectionately linked, the trees being a metaphor for memories, memories for trees. Unseen and unknown, the point of arrival is not strange but peopled with a past familiar only to the self, like Verlaine's ideal woman. Yet, seeking to establish the woman's name, Verlaine was satisfied to remember only its sound, "gentle and sonorous," and inquired no more. Char, on the other hand, determinedly confronts the woman in order to learn a name he once knew, and knows he knew, but must learn again. The answer he receives cannot surprise us for, as we have seen, the poem is written in the image of one who does not negate freedom or the errant innocence of a child but represents heedfulness at complete variance with any prescriptive order or naturalistic accounting; the glance measuring and distinguishing in the way we explore and come to know our delight; poetry conceived as love, love conceived as poetry. But there is a further resonance that is moral: the minutiae are not scattered pieces that make no sense; instead the woman reveals to poet and reader what they mean since flood, landscape, women are so many emblems of enduring grace despite the menace of mortality. Thus the last words convey no surrender but rather the achievement of a calm in which details have found their right and necessary place, fluidity a shore like that of the poem.

The single paragraph of "La Minutieuse" is a continuous whole that reaches a moral and poetic truth by way of seeming formlessness. This gradation constitutes a binary composition whereby a first section of thirteen sentences is followed by a second section of fourteen. Rhythmically they are distinct: in the first half we observe a series of metrical symmetries: three octosyllables, two decasyllables, three enneasyllables, two sentences of thirty syllables (if sentences 10 and 11 are taken together), and two sentences of thirty-seven. This unusual series of balanced groupings—some almost acrobatic, is the means whereby a lyrical movement sustains and patently imposes its measure. In the second half, on the contrary, isometry is almost entirely avoided: there are two octosyllables and two dodecasyllables, but the meter characteristically escapes rhythmic correspondence in proportion as feeling and thought themselves become more explicitly lyrical. This counterpoint runs parallel to a grammatical division that shows the use of the imperfect tense in the first half (only varied by two subjunctives) whereas the second half opens on two past definites ("s'arrêta," "continuâmes"), is punctuated by four others ("parut," "me rendis," "voulus," "endormit"), as well as by three pluperfects ("était demeurée," "avions atteint," "avait oublié"), a conditional ("retiendraient"), two presents ("ont," "suis"). The complex interplay of these tenses articulates a significant change in which description is joined to action, narrative to interpretation. Another feature of the dominant role of verbs in the second half is the presence of infinitives that explain, amplify, qualify ("pour causer et sourire," "de se montrer trop familière," "se montrer," "ne pouvait figurer," "cette façon de temporiser," "m'enquérir"). We are taken out of the domain of appearance into that of purpose and meaning. Without losing his grasp of the concrete, the poet shows by his composition that visual attention nourishes and penetrates the intellectual, the phrase "l'orée de très vieux arbres et la solitude des souvenirs" serving to illustrate a structural interconnection as pleasurable as a couplet.

Char has said that "le poème est toujours marié à quelqu'un."[42] We have no need to inquire into the private circumstances that surrounded the writing of this page and "married"it; whatever the source, we are moved by the concept of love as vital ambivalence, jubilant exchange.

[42] "The poem is always married to someone" ("Partage formel," *Poèmes et Prose choisis*, p. 219).

Waywardness and wisdom, fancy and restraint are complementary, like the descriptive and the intellectual, the
concrete and the abstract, the violent and the tender. And
this inclusive beauty is, we realize, coterminous with
Char's own poetry whose unfailing source is nature and
woman, and which, even when it evokes an ideal past,
speaks not from nostalgia but from the sense of time
redeemed.

La Paroi et la Prairie offers a high expression of Char's
work and its invigorating myth. Energy and brevity, concrete detail and abstract sense, make his poetry one of the
most forceful of our time. He finds the undissociated voice
of reflection and fervor, of thought pursued to its point of
peril, which calls to mind Yeats' words regarding the pos-
sessors of a fatal insight who by art are reborn: " . . . for it is
only when the intellect has wrought the whole of life to
drama, to crisis, that we may live for contemplation and
yet keep our intensity."[43]

Each of the ten pieces illustrates a revolt against stasis. In
the dark night of Lascaux and the sunshine of Provence a
frieze of animals participates in the timeless round. Orion
is not dead but among us, seeking out beauty, which is but
another name for the space and time of love. He takes his
inspiration from humble images, which become his means
of perceiving a goal that regenerates his commitment. "Ce
qui importe," Char writes, "c'est de fonder un amour
nouveau à partir d'êtres et d'objets jusqu'alors indiffér-
ents."[44] So the mortal meeting of man and bison is a privileged sign of reconciliation; black stags open the widening
circles of hope; the unnamable beast is an eternal attendant

---

[43] W. B. Yeats: *Autobiography*, New York, Macmillan, 1965, p. 183-184.
[44] "What matters is that a new love be founded on beings and objects
that have been hitherto indifferent" (*Recherche de la base et du sommet*,
p. 60).

of experience, who waits for men to grasp the true direction of their striving; the colt incarnates the alliance of
meditation and conflict; in "Transir" the poet-hunter is reduced to the most basic of his comforts but still envisages
victory, freely gives himself for the warmth to come. The
second section opens on the death of the bull that proposes
the convergence of love and truth; the trout is the fascinat-
ing image of the heart's limpid passion; the snake seeks
wisdom, shuns bombast, holds to awareness; the lark is
the fragile object of the hunt that inevitably dies when
brought to earth; and "La Minutieuse" is the epiphany of
Orion at one with nature, who accomplishes a migration
that registers each detail in the likeness of the woman by
his side, and thereby compounds the sum of love. Thus
the myth of desire is depicted, not after a uniform fashion,
but in accord with the discontinuous rhythms of a vibrant
creativity.

At no point do we feel that the individual pieces strain to
fit a plan, so that here Char's reference to the writer's freedom may be apt: "Le poète est la partie de l'homme réfractaire aux projets calculés."[45] Nevertheless, if the dialectic
of the hunt unfolds in apparently spontaneous manner,
we find a sure pattern that counterpoints the sequence.
The wall requires the prairie, the prairie the wall: complementarity prevails as the contained violence written
into "Homme-Oiseau mort et Bison mourant" and "Le
Taureau" is answered by the tenderness of stags and trout;
in the same way, the intellectual detachment of "La Bête
innommable" and "Le Serpent" is balanced by the instinctive exultation of colt and lark; and, finally, the laconic
heroism of "Transir" discovers its response in a splendid
narrative of grace. Each postulate demands the other, the
law of conscious responsibility calling on the presence of

---

[45] "The poet is that which in man is recalcitrant to calculated designs"
(*ibid.*, p. 36).

contrasting attitudes just as wall calls on prairie.[46] From the structure itself a poem emerges whose meaning is not only aesthetic but moral: articulating Char's quest for a language that is more than masterless hammer, the work becomes man's present and future—the token of the hunter's achievement, and the simultaneous oracle of that which yet can be attained by clear-eyed resolve and self-qualifying awareness. Such is the substance of *La Paroi et la Prairie*, which also informs the other pages of a poetry of concentrated power. The ambition for literature is extreme, like the enduring commitment that spans fifty years. As we read in *Fureur et Mystère*:

> Dis ce que le feu hésite à dire
> Soleil de l'air, clarté qui ose,
> Et meurs de l'avoir dit pour tous.[47]

and again, in the latest collection, the sheer tonicity of which—cold setting off warmth, image begetting symbol—is no less exigent:

> Refuse les stances de la mémoire.
> Remonte au servage de ta faim,
> Indocile et dans le froid.[48]

What Char offers in the nervous succession of his writings, I take to be the fulfilment of central preoccupations in modern French poetry. He has found antecedents in the anguish that stems from Baudelaire as well as in the spiritual quest pursued by the long line of visionaries since

[46] Cf. "Tour à tour coteau luxuriant, roc désolé, léger abri, tel est l'homme, le bel homme déconcertant" ("Le Rempart de brindilles," *Poèmes et Prose choisis*, p. 269). "Turn by turn lush hillside, desolate rock, light shelter, such is man, noble and disconcerting man."

[47] "Say what the fire hesitates to say / Sun of the air, daring brightness, / And die for having spoken for all" ("Dis . . . ," *Fureur et Mystère*, p. 166).

[48] "Refuse the stanzas of memory / Reascend to your hunger's thralldom / Intractable and in the cold" ("Dieux et mort," *Aromates chasseurs*, p. 25).

Rimbaud. Yet for him the end-term of myth and poem, however fleeting, is not Baudelairian beauty, or Mallarméan purity, or Surrealist convulsion, but the unquenched flame and raging stream of an absolute erotic union. A relationship is proposed by what he has termed a desperate audaciousness: from this "deux à deux" of natural signs[49] will result, not the destruction of base matter as in Mallarmé, but a marvel of plurality. Thus he writes: "Dans le chaos d'une avalanche, deux pierres s'épousant au bond purent s'aimer nues dans l'espace. L'eau de neige qui les engloutit s'étonna de leur mousse ardente."[50] Stone and water, fire and snow meet in furious confrontation. . . . His work achieves force and virtue from the mutual constraints of a sensibility sharp-edged and subtle, a strict intelligence, a consuming ethical concern.

[49] "Tout le mystère est là: établir les identités secrètes par un deux à deux qui ronge et use les objets, au nom d'une centrale pureté" (Stéphane Mallarmé: *Correspondance*, vol. 4 [1890-1891], ed. Lloyd James Austin, Paris, Gallimard, 1973, p. 293). "The whole mystery is there: to establish the secret identities by a pairing that gnaws at objects and wears them away, in the name of a central purity."

[50] "In the chaos of an avalanche two stones wed in their leap and were able to love one another nakedly in space. The snow water that engulfed them was amazed by their fervent moss" ("Nous avons," *Les Matinaux*, p. 194).

SELECTED BIBLIOGRAPHY

PRINCIPAL WORKS BY RENÉ CHAR:

Le Marteau sans maître, suivi de Moulin premier, Paris, Corti, 1945; revised editions 1945, 1953, 1963, 1970. *Fureur et Mystère*, Paris, Gallimard, 1948; revised editions, 1962; also, in the collection "Poésie," Gallimard, 1967.

Les Matinaux, Paris, Gallimard, 1950; revised edition, 1964; also, in the collection "Poésie," Gallimard, 1969, together with *La Parole en archipel*.

A une sérénité crispée, Paris, Gallimard, 1951.

Recherche de la base et du sommet, suivi de Pauvreté et Privilège, Paris, Gallimard, 1955; revised edition, 1965; also in the collection "Poésie," Gallimard, 1971.

Poèmes et Prose choisis, Paris, Gallimard, 1957.

La Parole en archipel, Paris, Gallimard, 1962.

Commune Présence, Paris, Gallimard, 1964.

Le Nu perdu, Paris, Gallimard, 1971.

Aromates chasseurs, Paris, Gallimard, 1975 (1976).

CRITICAL COMMENTARIES:

"René Char," Special Number of the review *L'Arc*, Aix-en Provence, 1963.

"René Char," Special Number of the review *L'Herne*, Paris, 1971.

"Hommage à René Char," Special Number of the review *Liberté*, Montreal, July-August 1968.

"René Char," Special Number of the review *World Literature Today*, Norman, Oklahoma, Summer 1977.

Blanchot, Maurice: "René Char," in *La Part du feu*, Paris, Gallimard, 1949; also, "René Char et la Pensée du neutre," *L'Entretien infini*, Paris, Gallimard, 1969.

Blin, Georges: "Préface" à René Char, *Commune Présence*, Paris, Gallimard, 1964.

Caws, Mary Ann: *The Presence of René Char*, Princeton University Press, 1976.

Caws, Mary Ann: *René Char*, Twayne, 1977.

Dupin, Jacques: "Préface" to René Char, *Le Monde de l'art n'est pas le monde du pardon*, Paris, Maeght, 1975.

Guerre, Pierre: *René Char*, Paris, Seghers, 1961.

La Charité, Virginia A.: *The Poetics and the Poetry of René Char*, University of North Carolina Press, 1968.

Mounin, Georges: *Avez-vous lu Char?* Paris, Gallimard, 1947. *La Communication poétique*, précédé de *Avez-vous lu Char?*, Paris, Gallimard, 1969.

Rau, Greta: *René Char ou la poésie accrue*, Paris, Corti, 1957.

Richard, Jean-Pierre: "René Char," in *Onze Etudes sur la poésie moderne*, Paris, Le Seuil, 1964.

INDEX

"A***," 21
"Accomplissement (L') de la poésie," xii
Action (L') de la justice est éteinte, xii, 13, 24
"A la santé du serpent," 33
"Alouette (L')," 7, 91-95
Apollinaire, Guillaume, xi, xvi; "Les Collines," xi
"Argument," 23
Aromates chasseurs, xv, 3, 4, 5, 6, 15, 16, 33, 47, 48, 69, 106
Arrière-histoire du poème pulvérisé, xv, 5, 42
"Arthur Rimbaud," 5
Artine, xii, 12-13, 16, 23
"Asciens (Les)," 33
"A une sérénité crispée," 3, 34, 99
Austin, Lloyd James, 107
"Avec Braque, peut-être, on s'était dit . . . ," 85

Bataille, Georges, 58, 63; *La Peinture préhistorique: Lascaux ou la naissance de l'art*, 58, 63
Baudelaire, Charles, 106, 107
"Bête (La) innommable," 62-69, 105
"Bibliothèque (La) est en feu," 214
"Biens égaux," 89
"Bouge (Le) de l'historien," 35-37, 42
Braque, Georges, 28
Brauner, Victor, 28
Breton, André, xii, 23, 95

Breuil, Henri, 52, 58, 62, 70, 72, 73; *Quatre Cents Siècles d'art pariétal*, 52, 70

Camus, Albert, xiv, 28
"Captifs," 7
Caws, Mary Ann, 13; *The Presence of René Char*, 13
"Cerfs (Les) noirs," 58-62
Claire, xiv
Cloches (Les) sur le cœur, xi, 7, 43, 61
Commune Présence, xv, 6, 7, 9, 11, 12, 17, 21, 23, 24, 81, 85, 88, 93, 94
"Commune Présence," 23-28, 32
"Compagnons (Les) dans le jardin," 34, 95
"Complainte du lézard amoureux," 9
"Contre une maison sèche," 74
"Cotes," 47

"Dans la marche," 88, 94
Dans la pluie giboyeuse, 31
"Débris mortels et Mozart," 28-31
"Déclarer son nom," 6
Dehors la nuit est gouvernée, xiii, 7, 11
"Dentelles (Les) de Montmirail," 93
"Dieux et mort," 106
"Dis . . . ," 106
"Dot (La) de Maubergeonne," 4
"Dyne," 31-32

"Eaux-Mères," 98
"Ebriété," 5
Eliot, Thomas Stearns, 17
    The Waste Land, 17
Eluard, Paul, xii, 79, 196
    Choix de poèmes, 79
Ernst, Max, 28
"Evadné," 12

"Faction du muet," 3
Faire du chemin avec . . . , xv
Fête des arbres et du chasseur, 93
Feuillets d'Hypnos, xiv, 7, 34, 41, 47, 87
"Flexibilité de l'ennui," xi
Fournival, Richard de, 51
    Le Bestiaire d'Amour, 51
"Front de la rose," 23
"Frontière (La) en pointillé," 47
Frye, Northrop, 3
    The Secular Scripture, 3
*Fureur et Myst*ère, xiv, 23, 106

Giacometti, Alberto, 28

"Haine du peu d'amour," 12
Heraclitus, 34, 98
Homer, 65
"Hommage et famine," 37-39, 42
"Homme-oiseau mort et Bison mourant," 53-58, 59, 105

"Instituteur (L') révoqué," 24

"Je me voulais événement," 24, 28, 31, 32
"Jeu muet," 11
"Jeune Cheval à la crinière vaporeuse," 69-74
"J'habite une douleur," 42-48

Laforgue, Jules, 7
La Tour, Georges de, 28, 40-41, 72-73
Lautréamont, Comte de, 34
Leroi-Gourhan, André, 53
Lettera amorosa, xiv, 16-23, 52
"Lombes," 4

"Madeleine à la veilleuse," 39-42, 45, 73
Mallarmé, Stéphane, 23, 42, 94, 107; *Œuvres complètes*, 94; *Correspondance*, 107
Malraux, André, 28
Mano, Guy Lévis, 52
Marteau (Le) sans maître, xvii, xv, 7, 12, 13, 34, 98
"Marthe," 98
Matinaux (Les), xiv, 107
Matisse, Henri, 9, 16
"Météore (Le) du 13 août," 34
"Minutieuse (La)," 80, 88, 96-104, 105
Miró, Joan, 28
Molière, 65
Monteverdi, Claudio, 17
Moulin premier, 25
Mozart, Wolfgang Amadeus, 30-31

"Neuf Merci," 93
"Neuf Poèmes pour vaincre," 37
Nietzsche, Friedrich, 34
"Nous avons," 107
Nu (Le) perdu, xv, 3, 11, 41, 47, 53, 74
"Nu (Le) perdu," 53, 74
Nuit (La) talismanique, xv, 33

"Orion iroquois," 5, 16, 69

"Parages (Les) d'Alsace," 11
Paroi (La) et la Prairie, xiv, xvi, 51-107
Parole (La) en archipel, xv, 29, 51
Partage formel, 26, 28, 35, 81, 101
Pascal, Blaise, 80
Picasso, Pablo, 28
Poe, Edgar Allan, 94
Poème (Le) pulvérisé, 42
Poèmes et Prose choisis, xv, 3, 7, 8, 9, 12, 13, 26, 28, 33, 34, 35, 37, 41, 47, 81, 87, 88, 93, 95, 101, 106
"Poings (Les) serrés . . . ," 24
"Pontonniers," 4
"Prêt au dépouillement," 43
"Progressivement sur la passe," 61

"Qu'il vive!," 9
Quatre Fascinants, 52, 88, 97

Ralentir Travaux, xii
"Réception d'Orion," 4
Recherche de la base et du sommet, xii, 5, 28, 33, 37, 39-40, 74, 104
"Redonnez-leur . . . ," 9
"Remise," 11
"Rempart (Le) de brindilles," 106
"Requin (Le) et la Mouette," 9-11
Reverdy, Pierre, 29
Rimbaud, Arthur, xii, xiii, 3, 26, 27, 29, 34, 98, 99, 107; *Illuminations*, xiii, 29, 80, 99
Rodin, August, 4
"Rodin," 4
"Rougeur des matinaux," 81

"Sade," 12
Saint-John Perse, xiii
"Serpent (Le)," 87-91, 105
Soleil (Le) des eaux, xiv
"Sorgue (La)," 98
Staël, Nicolas de, 28

Supervielle, Jules, 62
Le Forçat innocent, 62

"Taureau (Le)," 80-84, 85, 89, 91, 101, 105
"Tous compagnons de lit," 7
"Transir," 74-81, 105
"Transparents (Les)," 9, 87
"Trois (Les) Sœurs," 11
"Truite (La)," 84-87, 89
"Tu ouvres les yeux," 12

Valéry, Paul, 64-65
Van Gogh, Vincent, 70
Visage (Le) nuptial, xiii
"Visage (Le) nuptial," 13-16, 21, 23, 24
"Voici," 12
Voltaire, François-Marie Arouet, 98

Yeats, William Butler, 23, 104; *Autobiography*, 104

Zervos, Christian, 52
Zervos, Yvonne, 13, 53

PRINCETON ESSAYS IN LITERATURE

The Orbit of Thomas Mann. By Erich Kahler

On Four Modern Humanists: Hofmannsthal, Gundolf, Curtius, Kantorowicz. Edited by Arthur R. Evans, Jr.

Flaubert and Joyce: The Rite of Fiction. By Richard Cross

A Stage for Poets: Studies in the Theatre of Hugo and Musset. By Charles Affron

Hofmannsthal's Novel "Andreas." By David H. Miles

Kazantzakis and the Linguistic Revolution in Greek Literature. By Peter Bien

Modern Greek Writers. Edited by Edmund Keeley and Peter Bien

On Gide's Prométhée: Private Myth and Public Mystification. By Kurt Weinberg

The Inner Theatre of Recent French Poetry. By Mary Ann Caws

Wallace Stevens and the Symbolist Imagination. By Michel Benamou

Cervantes' Christian Romance: A Study of "Persiles y Sigismunda." By Alban K. Forcione

The Prison-House of Language: a Critical Account of Structuralism and Formalism. By Frederic Jameson

Ezra Pound and the Troubadour Tradition. By Stuart Y. McDougal

Wallace Stevens: Imagination and Faith. By Adalaide K. Morris

On the Art of Medieval Arabic Literature. By Andras Hamori

The Poetic World of Boris Pasternak. By Olga Hughes

The Aesthetics of György Lukács. By Béla Királyfalvi

The Echoing Wood of Theodore Roethke. By Jenijoy La Belle

Achilles' Choice: Examples of Modern Tragedy. By David Lenson

The Figure of Faust in Valéry and Goethe. By Kurt Weinberg

The Situation of Poetry: Contemporary Poetry and Its Traditions. By Robert Pinsky

The Symbolic Imagination: Coleridge and the Romantic Tradition. By J. Robert Barth, S. J.

Adventures in the Deeps of the Mind: The Cuchulain Cycle of W. B. Yeats. By Barton R. Friedman

Shakespearean Representation: Mimesis and Modernity in Elizabethan Tragedy. By Howard Felperin

René Char: The Myth and the Poem. By James R. Lawler

LIBRARY OF CONGRESS CATALOGING
IN PUBLICATION DATA

Lawler, James R.
  René Char : the myth and the poem.

  Bibliography: p.
  Includes index.
    1. Char, René, 1907-   —Criticism and interpretation.
PQ2605.H3345Z745   848'.9'1209   77-85547
ISBN 0-691-06355-9